Life in Lower Slaughter

Life in Lower Slaughter

Robert G. Deindorfer

Saturday Review Press | E. P. Dutton & Co., Inc.
New York

Portions of this book appeared in different form in *The New York Times*, copyright © 1971, 1974, by The New Times Company. Reprinted by permission.

LIBRARY OF CONGRESS CATALOGING IN PUBLICATION DATA

Deindorfer, Robert G
Life in Lower Slaughter.

1. Lower Slaughter, Eng.—Social life and customs.
2. Americans in England. 3. Deindorfer, Robert G.
I. Title.
DA690.L844D44   1975   914.2   74-23699

Published simultaneously in Canada by Clarke, Irwin & Company
Limited, Toronto and Vancouver
ISBN: 0-8415-0353-2

To
Joan and Scott
without whom this trip wouldn't have been
nearly so much fun

Life in Lower Slaughter

Chapter 1

The alarm clock went off all too early on Monday, July 9, 1973. For tactical reasons it stood just out of reach, up on a chest of drawers in a far corner of our bedroom, playing its daily tune—rackety, insistent, a maddening call to arms. The clock kept right on banging until it wound completely down.

"The only thing worse than waking up in the morning is not waking up at all—and I'm not so sure about that," a former colleague at the New York Stock Exchange used to say.

Exactly my sentiments. Besides, the last few days had been especially wearying. Caught in a narrowing time span, which was stretched to its limits by lists of things that had to get done, we'd been shuttling through the burning urban grid shopping, talking with bankers, insurance agents, and stockbrokers, visiting friends, attending parties, and uncorking a bottle for anyone who stopped by. If I didn't instantly respond to the alarm, well, I'd had less than a proper ration of sleep.

But once I came to, I would have shaved, dressed, and brushed what remain of my teeth a bit faster except for the usual obstruction. Our only full bathroom was densely populated with family. "It's hot again—hot and humid." The fresh T-shirt I'd skinned on was almost soaked through already. "Dear God, but it's hot." "Of course it's hot," my wife said. Unless she was under some fairly serious delusions, Joan apparently hadn't caught the name of the Party I was addressing. "It's always hot. What do you expect me to do about it?"

"Well, why not throw another log on the air conditioner?"

As we dressed, ingested a jiffy breakfast, and stuffed the last few downright necessities into our bulging suitcases, a radio treated us to the morning news. A fireman who had been injured in a blaze set off by a stray loony lay critically ill; a teenager confessed to shooting a neighbor dead and wounding three children; two men had been fatally stabbed in separate disputes; the long-running gravediggers strike—New York City was plainly in need of its gravediggers—was finally resolved. My stricken Yankees, the proud old dynasty only a memory now, had lost again.

A cursory inventory of the morning mail didn't exactly lift my spirits, either. Along with the usual free-enterprise mash notes, one of them a form hustle that I couldn't possibly do without a snowmobile, order form attached, the mail included still another prickly computer-spun threat from Internal Revenue. Ah well, the feds were having their last turn at bat for a while. All that luggage piled in the front hallway in no way meant that I was abandoning my familiar role as a patriotic pigeon forever paying taxes while I teetered on the edge of insolvency—an important point I want to make, what one prominent, if not beloved, six-figure tax audit victim would describe as perfectly clear. After all, I'd willingly be contributing at approximately the same rate elsewhere, which didn't bother me. But at the least the boys at IRS would have no reason to continue shelling me with insolent or-else letters, aside from force of habit, of course.

Once out our front doorway I rigged the customary security

4

measures. One, two, three separate locks bolted shut, and a heavy steel bar inside the door audibly clicked into place. As it happened, nobody in our apartment building had been burgled for more than a month, glory be, but this was no time to ease up.

In the spring and summer of 1973, the number of burglaries, rapes, muggings, and murders in New York was rising ominously. Alarmed by the figures and understandably nervous about walking the streets at night, more and more East Side Manhattanites in search of answers organized impromptu neighborhood meetings as a kind of group therapy. At one gathering of residents of East Seventy-first Street between Park and Lexington Avenue that I attended, little old ladies, button-down Wall Street businessmen, and bell-bottomed younger neighbors angrily spoke of "those people," and several asked about the legal problems of laying in clubs, rifles, and/or shotguns. Worse, a community-affairs specialist sent over by the New York police did nothing to diminish the skin-deep prejudice and the vigilante fever. "In case anything happens, just call me," he said. "Remember, you're defending your homes—and it's your word against theirs."

But there were even more immediate perils for us that particular morning. We loaded our suitcases on the small crap-shoot elevator, pressed the button, and hoped, hoped, hoped we'd make it to the lobby without stalling out between floors again. For the sake of novelty, perhaps, we did.

Outside the building the heat hit us like a wall; the temperature was eighty degrees and still climbing, and the accompanying humidity was so brutal my seersucker soon gummed to my body. Candy wrappers, soft-drink cans, and paper weren't all that covered the street. As I toddled off in search of a cab my carefully polished shoes skidded in the proof that the city was surely going to the dogs. Our devoted youngster whooped with laughter.

"Was it that rhino, Daddy?" he asked.

In New York City, in 1973, that was what passed as a quaint father-son joke. Several days earlier, in front of the health-food

5

shop on the corner, I'd been ambushed by a pile of fertilizer so abundant that Scott and I wryly got to wondering whether someone in the neighborhood owned a pet rhinoceros. Whatever it was, the beast hadn't been properly curbed.

"You weren't kidding." A cheery blond lady came down the steps of her brownstone. "You're really doing it."

"Indeed we are. And not a moment too soon. Several moments too late, in fact, as you can see." I scraped my fouled shoes against the curb.

"You're lucky. You're very lucky. If it weren't for Bob's practice, we'd do the same thing ourselves."

On Lexington Avenue a fat man swinging two attaché cases—maybe he packed his lunch to the office—scuttled out of a drugstore and beat me to an empty cab. Although my gorge predictably rose some, it was no day for a show of force. Instead, I confined myself to making a vulgar gesture. Five minutes later, I managed to get a cab myself, a big one too, a Checker, which wasn't quite the bonanza I'd expected it to be. Even before the driver started the meter running he launched into one of those cliché mister-I-been-hacking-thirty-five-years soliloquies. He turned left, left again, and then braked to an angry stop behind a garbage truck grinding in the middle of the street.

"Come on, move it." The driver leaned hard on the horn. "Move it, you spic bastard."

A line of cars piled up behind us while those urban noblemen, the sanitation workers, slowly lifted garbage cans off the curb, slowly wrestled them into the street, slowly emptied them in the back of the mother truck blocking our way. The driver and crew didn't so much as turn to acknowledge the deafening blare of horns.

Once the street finally opened up again, we hit the familiar track—York Avenue to Ninety-sixth Street, onto the crowded East River Drive, left up a ramp onto the Triboro Bridge. A string of barges rode the thick brown sludge washing far below.

The chronic wail of a police siren rose when we passed through the toll booth.

On the middle span of the bridge, outbound for Long Island, with our driver spinning tiresome personal reminiscences for the fascinating book he would write if only he had the proper connections, we turned for a farewell glimpse of the magical Manhattan skyline. It lay off to the right—the Empire State Building, the Chrysler Building, even the twin towers of the new Wor'1 Trade Center—the whole of it visible, faintly visible, through a grimy haze of pollution that looked very much like another Unsatisfactory Air Quality rating on the evening news.

During the drive out potholed Grand Central Parkway I skimmed the morning's *New York Times*, a gusher of disaster as usual, which reported a big heroin bust in the Bronx, another gypsy cabdriver slain, five riders competing in a championship bicycle race in Central Park attacked by thugs armed with clubs, chains, and knives. The news out beyond the city limits, in the land mass that Silent Majority Americans keep reminding everyone is far more typical, seemed no brighter. Convicts in Vermont held two prison guards hostage; Midwestern governors met to discuss the fuel shortage; the latest Watergate scandal reverberated; the rickety old dollar had depreciated 10 percent more in France, West Germany, and Switzerland in the past two weeks. It was enough to make a grown man swear off something or other —maybe even newspapers.

"Here's an odd one," Joan said. She quoted a story in the second section of the paper describing how four local drawbridges had jammed and locked in the brutal heat the previous afternoon.

At JFK Airport I began flinging devalued money around, $11.50 cab fare plus a $5 tip for the loquacious driver, who accepted it without making any thank-you noises; $2 for the skycap who trundled our nine pieces of luggage into the terminal; $27.40 for excess baggage weight; various amounts for cigarettes at the

7

duty-free shop, magazines at the newsstand, soft drinks at the snack bar.

If the sights and sounds around us were abrasive, it came as no great surprise. Voices from loudspeakers blankly announced delayed departures, children whimpered, outbound passengers snapped at airline employees, airline employees occasionally forgot the basic training manual and snapped right back. A thin little strip of a policeman briskly walked a wobbly drunk toward the building exit. Hidey ho, let's everyone have a wonderful holiday trip.

With a few minutes to spare before our flight boarded, I decided to call the midtown office where I'd done time for the last three years. Almost predictably, the coin box swallowed up my dime without giving me even the satisfaction of a dial tone. Another ten-cent investment put me through, after which I spoke with several friends, including my secretary.

"How are things now that I'm gone?" I inanely asked her.

"So far, so good. We haven't had to evacuate the building because of a bomb threat again—not yet, anyway."

When our flight w· called we submitted to the usual frisk of our hand luggage Vith skyjacking a perilous fact of life, the airlines couldn t be blamed for screwing security measures as tight as they could. As I filed through the photoelectric frame the warning buzzer squawked. A guard suspiciously patted me up and down, lifted the tangled ring of keys for all those locks back on East Seventy-first Street out of my coat pocket, and suggested I try again. Bingo.

One final indignity awaited us. Three other passengers holding identical numbers already filled the special seats—with a youngster in tow, it's nice to have facilities close by—an airline employee had assigned to us an hour before. A ruffled flight steward sorted things out exactly as I expected. We sat elsewhere, up near the front of the tourist-class section, almost as far from the facilities as possible.

Our plane waited its turn, taxied into position, and went thundering down the long track of runway. All of a sudden we were aloft, jet engines screaming, rising over diminishing rooftops and the metropolitan sprawl, climbing the dirty urban skies, lifting higher and higher, until the bittersweet city was only a speck out the window.

The filth and the throbbing heat, the traffic snarls and the itchy fear of violence, the insolence and the soaring price of everything, made that particular morning a day much like any other day in New York City, except for one thing. We were leaving— really leaving. We'd sublet the apartment, sublet a fishing cabin in the Catskills, sublet my round-the-calendar Tuesday night tennis, sublet season tickets for the Giants, the Jets, and Army football.

On Monday, July 9, 1973, we were fulfilling a wistful daydream. For better or worse, Joan, Scott, and I were forsaking Fun City and Fun Country for at least two specimen years abroad.

Chapter 2

Halfway across the North Atlantic on that first day of our informal exile, as the plane moved through blue skies at what the in-flight loudspeaker kept reminding us was an altitude of who really cares how many feet, a fellow traveler (how he'd hate even a literal use of the expression) from Ohio who was flying Old Glory in his coat lapel struck up a conversation as we stood waiting our turn at the rear of the plane.

"Be away long?" he asked me.

"It depends."

"Depends on what?"

"Nixon."

"Nixon?" His eyes slitted some. "What do you mean Nixon?"

"Well, we won't be coming home until he's out of office."

Despite a boiling long-running contempt for Nixon, my answer was false. We were pulling out for a variety of other reasons, both positive and negative, not the least of them a basic vagabond itch to pack off to somewhere else for a while. As intended, however, my provocative answer hit him right on the nerve ends. "Richard Nixon is a great president"—his voice lifted a few notches—"and a great American."

Otherwise the flight unwound along the same old lines, a nice woolly nap, two cardboard meals, stiffened kneecaps in the limited space. Far below, jigsaw pieces of land began to appear, first Ireland, then England, finally London, despite the foggy covering. The landscape looked bigger and bigger from the window until we became a part of it too, when the plane touched down with a thank-God grip on the landing strip.

At Heathrow Airport the culture shock we promptly experienced went far beyond our reaction to the resident stiff-upper accents. As we shuffled through the various stages of debarking we were treated to warmth, good manners, and humane consideration that we hadn't been accustomed to back where the flight originated. As we came off the plane, a fellow passenger, an Englishman returning home from a holiday in the United States, even insisted on carrying a piece of our hand luggage up the hellish long ramps to passport control, which was almost as big a breeze as customs.

"Anything to declare?" a cheery bureaucrat asked.

"No. Nothing."

"Carry on then."

As we whooshed straight past customs without the usual indignity of opening at least one bag, my supply of rather more tobacco than the law allowed still intact, I couldn't help but recall returning to America years before with my father after a European trip. An especially gung-ho U.S. customs agent—perhaps he had to meet a daily quota, like traffic cops used to in Riverside, Illinois—not only insisted on unzipping every piece of luggage we had but also suspiciously rummaged through their contents.

"My God, boy, next time I'm going to fill a bag with live Gaboon Vipers," my red-headed father sputtered.

Two London-based friends who generously had insisted on coming out to collect us stood waving beyond the final barrier at

Heathrow. A Cockney porter lifted our belongings onto a cart, wheeled them to the parking area, and carefully packed everything in our friend's car. He cheerfully thanked me for a tip of 40 English pence, or $1 U.S.*

Talking, talking, talking, catching up on the lost year since we'd last gathered together, we drove a dual carriageway across the Hammersmith flyover, down Kensington High Street, along the wall behind Buckingham Palace, to a comfortable old favorite of a hotel standing in a quiet mews. A night porter with a memory as long as his blotchy face affably greeted our son by name. Fresh-cut flowers and a bowl of fruit compliments of the manager awaited us in our room.

Up came sandwiches and milk for the youngest among us, sandwiches and something more appropriate for the graduates. A television newscast—reporting another scheduled trip by the prime minister, a Roman archeological dig near Cirencester, giving action replays on a golf match, predicting sunny spells tomorrow—had an innocent flavor until a jarring flash from offshore intruded. Watergate was erupting again. The last thing I remembered that night was the sound of a horse drumming on a cobbled street.

Next morning, there were promises to keep in London before we packed off again. Riding cabs and double-decker buses, occasionally risking the blind-side traffic pattern we hadn't yet adjusted to, we stopped at Hamley's toy store for Scott, Harrod's for Joan, Hardy Brothers for a ration of salmon flies for me. We were putting by the supplies that would help sustain us among the strangers in an antique land. By noon I'd almost worn a hole in my American Express card.

During a stroll through Hyde Park, which was immaculate

*For the sake of my sanity I'm converting dollars and sterling at an easy-does-it rate of $2.50 the pound throughout this book. During our sojourn the conversion factor fluctuated between a low of $2.18 and a high of $2.56, with an average of around $2.35. Hence the actual dollar equivalent is generally a bit less than the prices I cite.

and free of litter, we couldn't help but be impressed by the sight of natives stretched out in canvas chairs who had no visible concern that someone would rustle their shoes right off their feet if they happened to fall asleep. At a snack bar we learned some English English: popsicles are ice lollies. In an area known as the Serpentine, Scott molded sand castles, splashed in the water, and gulped orange squash with two instant friends on an outing with their nanny.

Later that afternoon, we poured drinks for a London publisher of our acquaintance who stopped by the hotel to say hello and ask if and when I expected to finish a book I was especially slow at writing. Later, we had a dinner, a boiled dinner, a proper English boiled dinner, with an effusive lady who plays Santa Claus to us on a year-round basis. Later still, I rang up a former New York tennis mate assigned to London by *Time* magazine several months before.

"Well, how do you like it here, Bill?" I inquired.

"Love it. We love it."

"Do you miss anything special?"

"Sure. Shooting holes in your backhand." He whooped with laughter. "Your forehand too, come to think of it."

Our rest stop over and done with, we caught a train from Paddington Station to the west of England the following morning. We fed on sausage rolls and potato crisps while picturesque scenes flashed outside our compartment window. Swans drifted on a flat sheet of water, schoolboys dressed in regulation whites played the slow leisurely rhythms of cricket, a blond girl took a chestnut hunter up over a practice jump out behind an old stone barn.

The morning newspaper I'd packed along carried a front-page story filled with shock and alarm. In a land of 51 million people the number of registered hard-drug addicts came to a total of 1,555. If we didn't have more than that just in postal district 10021 back in New York City an official recount was in order. That wasn't the only impressive figure in the paper. The entertainment pages listed fifty-two—fifty-two, count them, fifty-two—live, dramatic shows currently playing in London. On that same July day, glittering, no-business-like-show-business Broadway was offering theatergoers a choice of exactly nine.

The edge of our excitement was beginning to bulge as we passed Didcot and Reading and continued rolling west. Off to our left a church steeple appeared, slim and perfect, rising over a tiny village of two-story buildings. At Oxford a rental car stood waiting outside the rail terminal. After I refuse to say how many stops to ask directions of courteous people, a roundabout finally brought us to the road marked Woodstock.

Out beyond Woodstock lay the Cotswolds, the green land rolling into long soft hills that stretched for miles, the dry stone walls and honey-colored rural communities bright with sunshine, the scene so peaceful and still that a jaded American skeptic felt a rare catch in his throat. The countryside might have been painted by the British Travel Authority. Along the way a cock pheasant whirred into flight, a flock of lambs grazed a grassy field, the keep of a ruined old castle leaned against the sky.

Every few miles we paused to feel the pulse of the local economy. At the one cinema in Chipping Norton tickets sold for 40 pence, or $1 U.S. A quart of fresh strawberries near Steeple Barton cost 12 pence, or 30¢ U.S. In Stow-on-the-Wold Mr. Paish the barber had put his price up to 30 pence, or 75¢ U.S. On the basis of those early returns the poorboy budget we'd hopefully worked up before we left looked well within reach.

Twenty-eight miles from Oxford we turned off the old Roman Fosseway onto a narrow track of road. We drove slowly past the doctor's stone home, the manor house, and the small church and parked on the edge of the village green where several youngsters just sprung from school for the day came pelting over to greet our son. We had arrived in Lower Slaughter, Gloucestershire, United Kingdom, total population exactly 191.

A vagrant year-old memory stirred at the sight of the transatlantic camaraderie among the kids. I remembered that on a three-

14

week holiday in Slaughter the previous summer Scott and several resident youngsters ran, jumped, and whooped with delight while playing a pickup game of cowboys and Indians in a pasture strewn with bales of hale across the small stream winding through the village.

"Well, home again, home again—sort of." Joan's face creased in a happy smile.

"Right," I said. "Here we are, for better or worse, for poorer or poorer."

There it stood in the sunny afternoon, St. Kellen's, circa 1730, a three-story, five-room stone house under a steep slate roof, what the British call a tidy cottage, maybe a bit too tidy, our digs for at least two years. Too many weeds bloomed in the front garden, but the fuchsia bush standing near our doorway was magnificent, and some dahlias colored the bottom of our dry wall.

We stepped inside to find that several capital improvements we'd specifically ordered from New York City had been completed to our satisfaction. Wall-to-wall carpets covered the floors throughout; an electrical central heating system had been installed; the walls in what passes as the master bedroom had been replastered, spackled and painted white. On either side of the small working fireplace, which we expected to use for sputtering atmosphere, new oak built-in bookshelves rose to the ceiling.

Other more surprising, less commercial touches were also evident as we trundled luggage into the cottage. A neighbor with a broom, dust mop, and a Hoover had made it wonderfully tidy in the American sense of the word too. Anonymous donors had thoughtfully treated us to the bounty of their gardens—two vases full of flowers, a head of lettuce, a bowl of tomatoes, along with two bottles of milk and a loaf of the real stuff from the mill bakery.

Despite the diminutive size of our village, social life began crowding in that first afternoon. A next-door neighbor invited me to come kill some brute trout with him on his private water the next evening. A lady on the square asked if we'd like to attend

15

a church fete—food stalls, donkey rides, brass band, ladies soccer game—in nearby Guiting Power two days hence. A troupe of Morris dancers from Oxford was booked to perform on the village green on Saturday.

Thrushes, blue tits, and robins fluttered outside. A red-headed boy who delivered the evening papers stopped by to sign us on. A lady who lived up the road, a spinster, cheery and helpful, deaf as a post, worked a horse she was preparing for the coming hunt season.

"It's lovely, the whole thing, but I'm worn to a frazzle," Joan said after she finished emptying the suitcases and filling bureaus and closets.

"Same here," I agreed, after emptying the last bottle of sherry I'd locked away the summer before. "Let's pack it in early tonight."

But such was not to be. At that moment we learned of an urgent social commitment for that very evening, theater, live theater, a play at the primary school a mile away in Upper Slaughter, which several infant participants playing in our back garden insisted we attend. Self-conscious oh-look-at-Harold-in-the-Eskimo-costume home talents generally give me a good roaring headache, but tactically this one amounted to a command performance. After all, Scott would be a student at the same school in only a few weeks—and presumably a headline mummer himself the next year.

As things turned out, the homespun vaudeville was no better or no worse than I anticipated, which in no way constitutes a favorable notice. Scenery fell over, the players got to giggling, whispered cues rose to insistent shouts. But even the most demanding critic would have been forced to acknowledge that a six-year-old neighbor named Alison enacted the demanding role of a tree with stunning conviction, although the magic spell diminished some every time she turned, smiled, and waved an upper branch at our son.

Back at the cottage, Joan concocted a potluck after-theater

16

supper, which consisted of the gift lettuce, tomatoes, homemade bread and milk, plus two orders of fish-and-chips (at 18 pence, or 47¢ U.S., per order) that I collected at a takeaway shop in Stow. The fresh strawberries we sugared for dessert made me wonder whether Mr. Ferrari on Lexington Avenue back in New York City hadn't been taking advantage of my good nature.

Later that night, some minor cracks appeared in the blissful scene. The narrow steps of our staircase plainly hadn't been built for size 12 feet; I banged my skull, which, while not quite a size 12, happens to be substantial, on the low doorframe leading into the bedroom; and our one and only bathroom was crowded as ever when it came time for my evening ablutions.

Still, the sights and sounds of that first sample day made our future seem wildly promising. The last of the summer sun melted down over a far hill, and a wedge of moon slowly climbed the darkening sky. The soft country night did not pulsate with police sirens, boozy quarrels, or traffic snarls; there was nothing but peace and quiet.

"What are you thinking?" I asked Joan when we shut off the lights.

"I'm thinking it's idyllic."

"So am I, so am I."

Almost seven years after buying an English cottage, we were putting it to the ultimate test. On the basis of several brief holiday interludes we knew St. Kellen's in Lower Slaughter was a nice place to visit. But now we wanted to know whether it was an equally nice place to live.

Chapter 3

Seven summers before, at the end of another frustrating trip to the River Wye in Wales in pursuit of a big cock salmon, my wife Joan and I awarded ourselves a consolation prize by taking a leisurely potluck drive through the Cotswolds before we returned home to New York City. As things turned out, we acquired something more than the memories.

For almost a week we followed narrow back roads wherever they happened to lead us—without an itinerary, without any hotel bookings, without even so much as a map. We explored Wroxton and Chipping Camden, Snowshill and Darlingscott, Winchcombe and Upper Swell. Then, on our very last day behind the looking glass, we decided to chase one more dirt road to its source. In our small hired car we rode through a watercolor landscape so quiet we could hear the birdsong and, winding around a long curve, saw up ahead a village straight off an old print—Lower Slaughter.

Standing under speckled skies, the scene consisted of a grassy common, ornamental little gardens, mellow old stone homes, and a thin stream, which flowed from a classic mill race and was spanned by two wooden footbridges. It was the kind of hamlet Thomas Hardy once described as a "one-eyed, blinking sort of place." Even today I recall my first sight of Slaughter, about eighty-five miles north and west of London, as an emotional experience every bit as powerful as first love or hooking an Arkansas bass as long as my arm.

"Wouldn't it be nice . . ." Joan started to speak, paused, started again. "Wouldn't it be nice to have a summer home right here?"

"Wouldn't it, though," I said. "Except that we have an apartment in New York City we can't quite afford, a fishing cabin in the Catskills we can't quite afford, an old Bentley we can't quite afford, and here we are off on a vacation we can't quite afford, either."

"I know," she said softly. "I know."

Silent again, we stepped over one of the bridges, nodded to an amiable old boy in a deerstalker, and walked a footpath to the top of the village. At the mill race two grown men—fishing with worms, God forgive them—landed five small trout while we stood watching. From a small stone building beyond the waterwheel came the unmistakable scent, pungent and evocative, touching memories of a lost Midwestern youth, of homemade bread, a warm loaf of which we bought and devoured on the spot. If I went a little weak in the knees, it's because a man doesn't expect a miracle of loaves and fish any more.

Next thing I knew, there we were, in Bourton-on-the-Water, two miles away, in what the British call an estate agent's office, where an agreeable, if somewhat bemused, young agent seated behind a cluttered desk carefully tuned in on my windy inquisition.

"There's nothing, absolutely nothing, for sale in Slaughter," he informed us that first day. "There couldn't be more than fifty properties in the village, could there? And, as you might guess, they don't come onto the market very often."

The agent gratefully accepted an American cigarette and considered briefly.

"Of course, if you're in no particular hurry, we do get hold of the odd cottage every so often." He reached for a pencil. "Perhaps you can give me some idea of your requirements, the general price range, that sort of thing, and leave your name and address back in the States."

Quickly we ticked off our requirements: at least two bedrooms, a kitchen and living room, modern indoor plumbing and electricity, a garden out front, right on the stream, all for no more than $15,000 U.S. After converting dollars to pounds sterling on a pad, he thought the price sounded sufficient.

Back in New York City I initiated such a drumfire of letters to the estate agent confirming our enthusiasm as something more than a vacation romance that he simply couldn't ignore us. Every so often he answered to say that, while nothing had come onto the market yet, he was quite hopeful the ideal property would open up. The more Joan and I talked about a summer cottage in Lower Slaughter, the more possessed we became by the thought.

Appropriately the cable arrived on Thanksgiving Day that same year: SMALL TWO-BED AVAILABLE SLAUGHTER LETTER FOLLOWS. The letter and accompanying black-and-white snapshot included all the particulars. St. Kellen's was a freehold, more than two hundred years old; it was stone with leaded windows, a slate roof and tall chimney stack, two bedrooms, modern bath, kitchen and living room, a fireplace, hot-water system and electricity, three stories high, in fairly good condition, and just under $10,000.

By phone we got hold of a doctor fishing friend in Wales, what Izaak Walton called a brother of the angle, who agreed to drive his wife to Gloucestershire for a close-up inspection of the property, including that old slate roof, which he warned me might be what he called dodgy. Two days later he rang back. He spoke for six and one-half minutes with hardly a pause, the whole of it favorable; most emphatically, he said we ought to buy the cottage immediately before someone else put in a bid.

"As a matter of fact, Robert," he cleared his throat over the transatlantic wire, "the cottage seems so ideal for the two of you, and the price so fair, we were afraid someone else might come buy it. I took the liberty of giving the estate agent a binder in your name."

On the basis of that excessive reaction, not to mention the binder, which was a liberty we appreciated very much, we commenced numbing negotiations by phone, cable, and letter, which included a progressively larger circle of people as we went along. By the time everything reached the proper boil, we had dealt with the estate agent ($172) in Bourton-on-the-Water, a lawyer ($70) in Hereford, a mortgage company in Cheltenham, banks in both New York City and London, where we abruptly opened a modest account to facilitate mortgage payments, and a man at the British Consulate in Manhattan, who affixed so many red ribbons to an official deed that it looked as if I'd won the heifer competition at the Kane County Fair back in Illinois.

Thus we came to own an antique stone cottage we hadn't ever seen. Or at least we owned it with the help of the Halifax Building Society, which extended a fifteen-year mortgage at an initial rate of 7 percent after we had sent off a down payment of 30 percent of the purchase price. My father, a roaring old Anglophile ever since his one and only trip through England, was as overjoyed as we were.

Like other property buyers elsewhere, of course, we found that our initial purchase put us on a treadmill to other expenses, although, in our case, these burdens were scaled to a fairly small size. Even before our first trip to England as property owners the next August, the estate agent recommended certain basic repairs. In marched the plasterer, the painter, the electrician, the carpenter, to the total tune of $425.

That summer we commenced what was to become an annual drill for the next seven years. We flew to London, holed up long enough to do some theater, caught a train to Oxford, and drove a rented car to Lower Slaughter, where we unlocked the front door and explored the property. Nobody had exaggerated. The fact that we had an oak beam in the living room ceiling, more closet space than we expected, and a spot of grass out back couldn't be interpreted as anything less than a bonanza.

The only visible flaw was a light bulb, an unshaded light bulb at that, screwed into a socket in the middle of the living room ceiling, the height of which was only six feet six inches to start with. The light was presumably the work of some rustic elf who had preceded us. After bending low every time I crossed the room, I rang up an electrician who hurried out, removed the fixture, plastered over the hole in the ceiling, and presented me with a bill for 50 pence, or $1.25 U.S.

With a proprietary air we puttered in our garden, unlatched the front gate, strolled along the shallow River Eye, some twenty feet of which belonged to us under old Riparian law. At dusk some neighbors came by to invite us over for a high tea of meat and potatoes.

During a long conference on the proper care and feeding of the house with our estate agent next morning, he ticked off several suggestions. Among other things, he thought the fireplace might be enlarged, weatherproofing laid on the ground floor, the far walls of the kitchen patched and replastered.

"Oh, and a cottage this age really needs people about," he said. "If you don't mind another suggestion, you ought to let it; no problem, either, not in Slaughter. People living in it will keep the old walls warm through the winter."

Since a rental could also help keep our family budget a bit warm too, we agreed to rent out the cottage provided the tenants he found would agree to vacate the premises in July and August of each year. With Lower Slaughter the most desirable village for miles around, the agent anticipated no problems arranging to clear it for us in the summer.

"Mind you, you'll have to furnish the cottage first," he told us.

In the case of unfurnished houses, possession by the tenant amounts to ten points of the law in England. Probably the most poignant case history we heard about this landlord-tenant relationship concerned an innocent young couple from West Germany who bought a relatively small fifteenth-century castle near Nottingham. Realizing that it would take them at least a year to sort out their affairs back in Germany, they rented it, without the precaution of furnishing it, to an English couple blessed with enough children—eight of them, as I heard the story—to fill up the castle. But when it came time for the Germans to reclaim their property, they found that the tenants had established the sort of legal squatter's rights that hold up in court, or did for two years of costly litigation—emphatic proof, I suppose, that a man's castle isn't necessarily his home unless he scatters a few sticks of furniture around before hanging out the "To Let" sign.

Thus Joan and I went visiting nearby antique shops in search of the beds, tables, chairs, dressers, sofa, wardrobes, and other essentials—splendid old oak, much of it, which we happen to like —at a total cost of $2,100. It doesn't take much furniture to comfortably fill a cottage whose living room is only twelve-by-sixteen feet.

In the end the rent paid by the two schoolteachers who inhabited the cottage for ten months of the year covered our annual mortgage payments and our property taxes. Although the teachers never did as much with the garden as we had hoped, or as one waspish neighbor personally told them they ought to, they were agreeable tenants, reliable and thoughtful, who didn't mind emigrating south to Spain every summer. For a commission of 7 percent of the rental figure, the estate agent collected the rent and sent it along to our London bank, which then settled the mortgage obligations on a quarterly basis.

During that first summer we managed to learn the proper use of the language: first floor for second floor, power points for wall sockets, dustbins for garbage cans. As New Yorkers accustomed to far more regular sanitation service, for all the rackety noise at daybreak, we also learned a bleak fact of life. In Slaughter the dustmen only stopped by every second Thursday, although the schedule eventually was stepped up to a weekly call.

Over the next few summers at St. Kellen's we added a larger refrigerator, a new sink, more lighting, a space heater, an epic double bed, some old pewter, brass, paintings, and an Oriental rug without too much mileage to it. Altogether, we payed out a total of just over $6,500 in five years, including that initial payment on the house itself.

Even the suffering moon-faced man who prepared our U.S. Internal Revenue forms beamed when he first looked into the economics. With a few bold strokes of his crayon he converted the cost of some repairs, furnishings, and essential restoration on the property into legitimate tax deductions. And as a writer frequently researching an article or a new book in Oxford, London, or Wales, I found that there were other tax advantages to be extracted from our summer trips to England.

American friends seemed so intrigued by our divided life style that I concocted a brief article about our inexpensive vacation three thousand miles away. Generally, any reader mail aimed in my direction consists of a few quarrelsome letters. But I hit a personal gusher with this one, 147 letters, from New Haven to Kansas City, professors and lawyers, bureaucrats and car salesmen, architects and businesspeople, including a doctor living three blocks from us in New York City. It was a random sample of fellow dreamers, every one of them wheedling me for more details, most of them asking for the name and address of the English estate agent we dealt with, which I volunteered in a form reply, to the distress of the agent himself, as I subsequently learned, if only because he felt obliged to answer the mail despite a very limited supply of properties available for sale.

Along with the strangers who merely read about our experience, several vagabond friends actually saw the cottage close-up during visits to England. One of them came to share our view to such a point that he began looking seriously for a similar cottage somewhere in the area.

But, then, he had every reason to react that way. The first week he spent in Lower Slaughter, Mrs. Gazzard, a jolly, generous soul who lives a few houses upstream from us, stopped him as he was strolling to the mill for a loaf of bread fresh out of the oven.

"You're an American, aren't you?" Mrs. Gazzard inquired.

"Yes. Yes, I am."

"I thought so. Well, hold on a moment now."

With that she scurried into her stone home, returned shuffling a handful of worn old picture postals of Times Square and Niagara Falls, the Washington Monument, and Cape Cod.

"Poor boy," she told our friend, who happened to be having the time of his life, "you must be homesick. These pictures may cheer you up."

For ourselves, we began to lean on our rural memories of July and August right through the urban year. We remembered side trips we made to Warwick Castle, Stratford-on-Avon, Bath, the Devon coast, Banbury, Tewkesbury, Shropshire, and the Wye Valley in Wales. We were within easy reach of the most magnificent, most comfortable old coaching inn in the country, the Lygon Arms in Broadway, not to mention a scaled-down version named Lords of the Manor in Upper Slaughter, where we put up any surplus American guests who wouldn't fit into our limited space and also treated ourselves to an occasional dinner.

Gradually, summer by summer, we also adjusted to the easy pace of village life. We attended services in the small church, politely applauded our local side in its weekend matches on the cricket pitch, and tramped through the countryside. The natives didn't seem especially restless to have us among them in the summers. We fraternized with several who invited us over for tea, cocktails, or dinner, especially a friend right next door, Walter Clifford, a vigorous retired gentleman farmer, who owns three large quarries stocked with trout, a mile on the nearby Dickler River, and a half-mile of salmon water near Hereford. Blessed with a neighbor like that I was no longer forced to lapse into the lurid exaggerations so endemic among ichthyologists. After all, the literal truth was hard to improve on.

Meanwhile, the quality of life we endured the remaining ten months a year in Manhattan continued tailing off. Under a noxious cloud of metropolitan smog, with police sirens and ambulances providing round-the-clock background music, subways growing slower, grimier, more crowded, and legitimate theaters, magazines, and favorite restaurants shutting down, the buoyant old spirit that had sustained New Yorkers through many an earlier crisis flattened into a futile whine. Scaled to size, similar agonies were apparent on visits to Aurora, Illinois; Columbia, Missouri; and Jacksonville, Florida.

Alarming fissures in the American society were plainly beyond the plastic gifts of a Nixon-Agnew ticket, which rode into office on the basis of—it seems almost comic in view of what was to come—a platform of Law and Order. Sullen America: Love It or Leave It signs appeared on more men's room walls, more car windows, more hardhats. Suffering minority blacks demonstrated the principal of a fundamental physical law: anything bottled up for too long is bound to explode. In Vietnam a cracked sense of national honor led to massive or-else bombings, secret wars in adjoining lands, and official high-level deceit.

Our cost of living went up, up, up—$850 advance tuition for nursery school, $950 for the periodontist, $1,800 annual dues for a basic necessity fishing club. Everything inflated except my own income, which, in fact, remained much the same, as our accountant bleakly reminded me on several occasions.

It seemed to me that a disproportionate number of personal friends, in and out of New York, were afflicted with ulcers, heart conditions, and mental problems so severe they required psychiatric treatment. Certainly, all too many married couples we knew participated in the rising national divorce sweepstakes. Two troubled, privileged, drugtaking young men whose parents I've known most of my life failed in attempts to kill themselves. An especially close friend who put a gun to his head one dark night didn't.

The rising pattern of urban violence, so staple an item in

26

television newscasts and on the front pages, remained an ominous threat. After experiencing not one but two muggings—the first required a total of twenty-seven stitches in the emergency room—a couple we liked enormously well fled to the Westchester suburbs out beyond our orbit. Other friends packed off for Connecticut, Long Island, New Jersey, Boston, Virginia, Washington, D.C., and California.

Under the circumstances, I don't suppose our one and only child could be blamed for a shattering remark after tracking the news on television early one evening: "No murders today, Daddy." Was there any way of restoring his innocence and sense of wonder? More than almost anything else, we hoped so.

As the pressures piled up and the old bounce of New York City diminished, a glimmer of an answer that must have been bubbling in my subconscious for some time surfaced as I fished an English quarry one soft evening during our annual vacation trip abroad. Everything spun by in slow motion: two cows grazing a field on the far edge of the water, some swans, several ducks, an occasional trout rippling the surface. But I returned to the cottage sooner than I had originally planned.

"Joan, I'm serious now, mind you, why don't we come live here in England for a couple of years?" I said. "We would manage. We could probably manage very well. You know me, have typewriter, will travel."

She screwed her face in concentration for a long while. Finally, a happy beam of approval appeared. "Why not? We've nothing to lose but our accents."

We talked of little else for the remainder of that vacation and through the early autumn. Even our youngster seemed agreeable. We fiddled with lists, wondered exactly what people in small English settlements did in the dead of winter, and fixed some optimistic sublet prices for our apartment, fishing cabin, indoor tennis series, and season football tickets. We'd commence eating high off the lotus the following summer.

However, at about the time we planned to make an official

announcement, two developments, one of them heartbreaking, the other merely frustrating, let the air out of our immediate plans. A succession of increasingly painful, increasingly serious illnesses beset my father, an aging widower who lived by himself, before he released his soul that next autumn on the kind of golden afternoon he used to love to drive the back roads of Illinois. As the senior surviving son, a number of melancholy responsibilities kept me shuttling out to the Midwest after his death as well.

Then I learned that I really couldn't jump the remainder of a three-year contract as an indentured servant with a Manhattan financial public-relations firm where I sat composing rhetorical nosegays on behalf of clients as diverse as the people who package Uncle Ben's Rice, a fleet of supertankers, and America's kindly one-stop, full-service bankers. I kept on hitting the spacebar for another season: "You'd never guess what Richard Porter locked in his $8-a-year safe deposit box at a full-service bank in Milwaukee. . . ."

As the months went on, the gloomy shape of events persisted. Various economic game plans failed to put a dent in bulging prices; the sinus in my right frontal lobe got to sorely throbbing. Along with everything else, the choice between two droning mediocrities like Nixon and McGovern, the latter to whom I perversely contributed more than we could afford, struck me as farcical in a country of more than two hundred million people.

Once we fixed a specific departure date, July 9, 1973, which seemed as good as any, responsibilities began stacking up. We made airline bookings, signed lease forms to sublet the apartment and other encumbrances, and contacted the shipping people to see how long before our decampment we'd have to start packing crates of books, toys, and fly rods. Joan even received a gift box of letterhead stationery inscribed with our future address right down to the GL54 2HS postal code.

Bills settled, official change-of-address cards mailed out, crates and trunks already shipped, our status as lame-duck New Yorkers became so obvious that a few skeptical acquaintances finally realized we didn't plan to back off at the last minute. One of them chose to cast our motivation in wholly negative terms during an abrasive conversation.

"I know why you're bugging out," he said. "Oh, to be in England now that Armageddon's here. Right?"

"Wrong. That's not the reason." I picked my words carefully. "Or at least that's only part of it, and not the most important part, either. The thing is we've fallen head-over-heels for Lower Slaughter."

And so we had. But now that we'd actually moved into our antique mortgaged cottage three thousand miles away from the Met and the Mets, from Brooks Brothers and Brooks Roberts, we couldn't be absolutely, positively, beyond-a-reasonable-doubt certain that we had made the right decision. Only time would tell. Time and my queasy aversion to beef-and-kidney pie.

Chapter 4

Once we adjusted to the leisurely local pace, the three of us took in some long-forgotten rural pleasures. We hiked, picnicked, wheeled our bikes along back roads winding nowhere in particular. After years of another form of bird watching, I learned to distinguish raven from crow, lark from thrush. A neighbor with a gift for folk medicine taught us how to dampen the hellfire of the stinging nettles we often walked into by rubbing dockleaf, growing in almost the same profusion as nettles, on our arms and legs.

The rolling countryside all around offered something more than the succulent blackberries we gathered to sugar and top with double cream. After we packed Christmas gifts—old pieces of silver and pewter, prints, and antique breadboards—off to friends and relatives back home, we walked along a stone wall at Copse Hill picking glazed holly in berry. Cows were herded into stone sheds to be milked, then driven out to night pasture. The sound of horses on tarmac roads, steady, hollow, almost liquid, soon became as constant as the urban noises of nighttime Manhattan. Except for the sheep, sheep, sheep, their fluffy hides marked with proprietary red, green, or black patches, grazing the wolds in every direction, the rural scenery brought me all the way back to those lost summers on a family farm near Lisle, Illinois.

It wasn't long before even significant dates we'd always set out on the calendar went out of focus. I had a suspicion this might be happening when what adults call Guy Fawkes Day and youngsters call Bonfire Night approached. For weeks resident children were out scrounging cardboard cartons, wood, and other combustibles to pile on the growing bonfire in a field behind the bakery. As usual, a few of them, including our son, displayed a casual sense of property rights while they gathered the ingredients. At least two bales of hay came out of a farmer's barn, and several lengths of lumber were removed from a construction site. The general mood of Guy Fawkes Day is rather like Halloween. Perhaps the victims of those and other excesses didn't really mind, although I felt they had little choice in the matter.

As the bonfire stack grew higher, higher, higher, reports filtered in from other precincts. Reliable sources spoke of larger piles in Bledington, Salford, Stow, and Chipping Norton. We could see for ourselves that the bonfire in neighboring Upper Slaughter, whose smaller population assays more boypower, was more impressive than our own. Driven by competitive furies, the kids took to foraging more and more raw materials, such as a moldering railway tie I'd filed away in our back garden to have split into kindling for the fireplace.

At six o'clock on Guy Fawkes night the baker's son put a torch to the ten-foot bonfire topped with a scarecrow figure labeled Guy, and some forty-five people, stomping their feet against the cold and warming their hands as the fire blazed, went into the traditional celebration. Hot baked potatoes were passed around; children drank cups of soup; adults quaffed beer and ale; pinwheels, sparklers, sky rockets, and Roman candles rose in the dark November sky. The light of that prodigious Upper Slaughter fire showed beyond a fold of shallow hills to the north.

As things turned out, attendant casualty figures awakened old echoes of July Fourth in the wild old years. A six-year-old boy screamed and clapped hands to his ears when a rocket exploded too close. A teen-age girl suffered powder burns holding onto a firecracker longer than she should have. An adult whose presence of mind is otherwise astute made the mistake of picking up a dead sparkler before it cooled off, which sent me straight home for ointment and a Band-aid, or what the British call a sticky-plaster.

A few weeks later Joan and I joined friends at Lords of the Manor in Upper Slaughter for a memorable feed of smoked salmon, thick soup, sirloin steak, and chocolate soufflé, which the pastry chef ought to have been knighted for. As we sat there still groaning from the meal, the genial hyphenated innkeeper stopped by the table.

"A pleasant Thanksgiving, was it, Mr. Deindorfer?" he inquired.

"How's that?"

"A pleasant Thanksgiving. Your American Thanksgiving, you know. Today is your American Thanksgiving."

It was the first Joan and I had realized it. If I felt a belated wrench, it wasn't for the traditional drumstick so much as it was for the traditional Green Bay-Detroit Lions football game on television.

As might be expected, the annual holiday cycle in England calls for some adjustments on the part of immigrants from America. Memorial Day, July Fourth, Labor Day and all those melting-pot nationality jubilees where ethnics put on funny hats and go parading up the avenue to the wild beat of the Our Lady of Victory school band simply don't exist. But the English do have something we ought to adapt for recuperative purposes, bonus days, two of them, one the day after Easter, the other the day after Christmas, official bank holidays enabling celebrants to unwind before they pick up the routine pieces of their lives again.

The backland British flavors we gradually absorbed that first year also included a number of fund-raising teas, jumble sales, and fetes, which vary in size. A full-blown fete can be an elaborate production. Scheduled to help diminish the chronic deficit of a church, civic club, or village council, a major fete consists of such components as a fancy dress parade and pony or donkey rides for children, darts, raffles, tambolas and other games of chance, an exhibition cricket or soccer game, and countless stalls where home-baked cakes, pies, and bread, fresh lettuce, tomatoes, berries and runner beans, hand-knit mittens, caps, and sweaters contributed by members of the sponsoring group are on sale at oh-boy prices.

When our local church fete in the Village Hall approached, we didn't know quite what to offer to help stock the stalls. Joan doesn't embroider and we don't have a kitchen garden. After reflecting some, however, Joan finally baked a banana cake out of the *Good Housekeeping Cookbook*, and I caught two nice trout out of a nearby quarry, which sold for one pound, 20 pence, or $3 U.S.

The commercial success of those trout taught me a lesson I badly needed to learn. Fresh fish amount to coin of the realm. In a land where adults not blessed with game-fishing water of their own must pay fairly stiff prices to lease beats from those who are blessed, trout and salmon amount to genuine luxury items. Accordingly, we began to work off obligations piling up for too long. In six productive weeks I presented surplus fresh-caught trout from as far away as the River Test to a total of sixteen people who had generously staked us to pheasant, artichokes, berries, peas, and other home-grown produce.

Among the beneficiaries of my Number 14 Hairwing Coachman was an elderly lady with a bad leg whose name I don't know to this day. Every so often she appeared outside the office space I rented two miles away in Bourton-on-the-Water, knocked on the window, and, explaining that "these are for your wife," whom she'd never met on even an informal basis, handed me bouquets of mixed flowers, red roses, and, on one occasion, a bag of raspberries. Late in the season I asked whether she liked trout.

"Oh yes, indeed we do. My husband and I love trout, baked in foil wrap, you know, stuffed with celery and pepper. But we hardly ever have them."

"Well, one never knows for certain, but if you come by tomorrow morning I might have a surprise for you."

I fished a long time that evening in an effort to balance out the supply-demand factor. Next morning when she came tapping on my windowpane, I gave her a brace of rainbow trout, lovely fish, too, if I do say so, firm, in splendid condition, each of them more than two pounds. The floral contributions came in with even greater frequency after that.

Gradually, without realizing it was happening, the three of us found ourselves caught up in an eddy of minor civic events. Scott rapped on doors selling tickets for the school sale, a fund for handicapped children, and a wildlife do-good. Joan contributed flowers to the church, a jug of wine to a benefit for a retarded child, that banana cake and other baked goods to various sales.

Soon after we arrived, or shortly before the natives got to know me for the paperwork tiger I am, I was elected—unanimously, let's nobody offend the Yank amongst us—a member of the Lower Slaughter Village Hall Committee. It was chaired by Sir Anthony Milward, who lived just across the stream from us, a career mogul whose formidable background banging the gavel included a long stint as chairman of BEA. Perhaps my belated political career was beginning at the required grass-roots level. As a regular communicant, I was also asked to read one of those Here Beginneth lessons at St. Mary's Anglican church and to perform other petty ecclesiastical duties.

Late that first year I even gave two public speeches—or, more accurately, I gave one speech on two different occasions. An acquaintance whose daughter acts as our baby-sitter recruited me to talk before his Rotary Club chapter in Stow. Since I invariably tend to choke addressing more than ten people, I was about to decline with the usual regrets when I heard the magic words "on any subject you want," which put a different light on the situation. As a student of intelligence and espionage, I've written magazine articles, books, and syndicated newspaper features, lectured, appeared on radio and television, and bombarded the public with cloaks and daggers in every conceivable way except beating on a hollow log.

I dusted off the same speech I'd often inflicted on American audiences, sent a dark suit out to the nearest presser fifteen miles away, and rehearsed a few mechanical gestures in front of the bathroom mirror. Despite the language barrier my speech was such a success that several natives who'd gotten wind of it subsequently phoned to ask whether I was willing to perform for their organizations. Among the invitations was one from a good friend right next door, to whom I was and am deeply beholden for a number of reasons, not the least of them frequent fishing on his private waters, who wanted me to address a fraternal order of retired business and professional men who gather together every second week at the Old New Inn in Bourton.

"Well, yes, Walter, maybe I can," I allowed. "I'd probably want to base my remarks on the talk I gave the Rotary, not the same speech, not the same speech at all, mind you, but along those general lines. Are any of your people members of that Rotary Club?"

"I don't believe so. But let me make certain."

He later confirmed the fact that there were no duplications and we were on. At the risk of sounding something or other, the talk went quite well for a while, with an audience of more than fifty British geriatrics, several so infirm I lifted my voice a notch in case the juice in their hearing aids was running down, smiling and expressing interest in the proper places. But halfway through a worn recitation that hadn't altered by so much as a moreover for five seasons, I noticed a rubicund moustached old-timer nodding in a far corner of the hall, his picturesque face

35

locked in my memory, unmistakenly a member of the Rotary Club audience. My hairline composure cracked. Gulping some, unable to take my eyes off the poor double-jeopardy victim there in the corner, I lost track of the familiar text and even repeated a line. Finally, a flash of understanding showed in his red face. He smiled and gave me a reassuring thumbs-up signal, which helped me through the remainder of it.

"Is the family orator planning any more speaking dates?" Joan politely inquired on learning of the calamity.

"Not anywhere in Gloucestershire, I'm not. And I don't expect to be in demand anywhere else."

It may have been wild coincidence, but invitations to speak elsewhere right in Gloucestershire dried up completely.

Meanwhile, as the seasons slowly unfolded, the elemental Our Town pattern of life continued. A baby girl was born to the baker's assistant and his wife; the schoolmarm married precisely the man her friends hoped she would; the vicar died and was laid to rest in the cemetery alongside the small sixteenth-century church where he'd interpreted the Word of God for so long.

Social notes in nearby Upper Slaughter, which, with a total population of merely eighty-six people, is even smaller than our village, documented the fact that life has its darker side out in rural England, too. One of the nicest youngsters in our son's school has no official father; a bouncy attractive young wife packed off to play house with an electrician whose own spouse wasn't being true blue; the string of extramarital conquests an especially kinetic local stud ran up was reported to include his buxom mother-in-law. Clearly, the natives take off their pants one leg at a time same as anyone else.

It wasn't long before our original suspicion that the isolation of the village might become oppressive faded away. While Lower Slaughter is indeed remote, a fly-speck settlement marooned on the edge of memory, it is warmed by the nearness of a number of neighboring villages little different one from another. Twists of country road lead to Notgrove, to Northleach and Wyck Rissington, to Cold Aston, to Clapton-on-Hill and Shipston-under-Wychwood. Unlike many dying communities we used to pass in New York State, where the only flourishing local industry appeared to be the fellow who paints all those For Sale signs, these British villages flourish still, gardens trimmed and bright, stone cottages filled with people, church steeples rising over the slate rooftops, cows milked, pigs and sheep fattened to the point of their doom, grain sown and harvested on adjacent farms that sustain the backland economy.

Picturesque little communities spin on for centuries without ever attracting any attention unless an exceptional occurrence suddenly lifts them onto front pages and television newscasts for a flickering moment of celebrity. Next-door Stow experienced just such a moment a few months after we had settled in.

On frequent trips to the greengrocer, the butcher, and the library in Stow we felt the wind of a civic controversy involving a magnificent old elm shading two benches and a relic wooden stock in the village square. After the parish council voted to have it cut to the ground in the interest of public safety, conservationists held rackety protest rallies, circulated petitions, and unfurled Save The Elm signs big as bedsheets outside homes adjoining the square. On the scheduled day of execution, a nimble dissenter scrambled high up into the tree and refused to budge until the council agreed to postpone the cutting and have some branches lopped off instead.

One final ingredient remained for the rural dispute to hit the national headlines. A local contractor, who happened to be celebrating his twentieth birthday, was crushed to death in the fork of the elm by one of the branches he'd been hired to trim. Inflamed fellow townsmen couldn't be blamed for practically tearing the diseased tree down with their bare hands, although the victim's father lent a proper professional touch to the felling.

37

Driving past a week or so later, we noticed several sprays of fresh flowers on the stump.

"Do you suppose those are in memory of the young man or the tree?" I asked.

"Both," Joan said, blinking a bit.

As we quickly learned, Slaughter is isolated, but without suffering any glaring lack of basic conveniences. Every morning the dairyman delivers enough bottled milk to keep our growing boy afloat. During the week a well-stocked mobile library, a lorry from a specialty food shop, and two butchers who cut fresh meat to order on wooden blocks in their curb-service trucks make regular stops. At dusk we listen for the tinkle of the ice cream wagon. Both mornings and afternoons a small red Royal Mail van comes rolling into the village square, and a surprisingly incurious postman passes any letters through our kitchen door.

"I expected they'd be wanting my advice again," I remarked once in an attempt to rattle his diffidence.

"Who's that you mean, sir?" he asked.

"The White House—who else?" Although it contained nothing more than a canned news release distributed to hundreds of journalists and writers, the large franked envelope the postman had just delivered was marked The White House, Washington, D. C. "Didn't you notice?"

"No, I didn't." His dark eyes bulged some as he verified the return address. It was obvious he hadn't noticed, which I found refreshing, if only for the sake of novelty. Back home the letter carriers I've known not nearly as well as they knew me included civil servants like silver-haired old Mr. Farr, who not only read the open mail he passed along View Street in Aurora, Illinois, but often even commented on the contents as well—as he did the morning he handed my mother a postcard with a hearty "Glad to see your sister is feeling better."

Along with those and other regular services, the occasional call for help doesn't go unanswered long in our remote village, either. As yet we haven't suffered a blizzard, a flood, or a bombing by the IRA crazies, but in the normal sort of emergency the appropriate people—doctors, veterinarians, fire fighters, television repairmen—seem to materialize from Stow or Bourton, without stopping for tea along the way. An impressive example of this jiffy response in times of crisis unfolded the Sunday night the electricity abruptly shut off in every cottage on our side of the stream, an inconvenience, needless to say, especially with a televised replay of the World Cup soccer final almost upon us, but nothing really serious. After all, we'd grown accustomed to occasional brownouts, power failures, and even the master grid lighting the whole northeast United States melting down back in Con Ed country. If the cause of this calamity was fairly exotic by Manhattan standards—a myopic swan had flown into the power line behind the mill, his remains on display for all to see—the cure was equally prompt. Within twenty minutes, an emergency crew from the Midlands Electricity Board unloaded a lorry and started stringing up a new wire.

In case it's ever more art, more modern times, more civilization we happen to feel a need for, we don't have all that far to go. These pleasures are to be had in other areas less than twenty-five miles away—the Royal Shakespeare Theater in Stratford, live theater and good music in Cheltenham, theater, symphony, and sometimes ballet in Oxford, not to mention counterculture frozen Sara Lee cakes, Wimpy hamburgers, and a bulging eyesore of a Hilton Hotel.

Any time an onset of the rustic bends calls for more powerful medicine, a fairly rare occurrence, incidentally, we learned we need only to book a healing trip to London, an ultimate urban bonanza offering more of almost everything we enjoy than even New York City, only an hour and forty minutes away by British Rails, a trip which in itself is invariably an agreeable experience. Trains are clean, prompt, and, despite an across-the-board increase enacted before our first year ran out, still relatively inexpensive. At times the trip brims with adventure—a steward serving genuine canapés, a man selling boxes of strawberries, an unscheduled mercy stop to avoid hitting some stray cattle—not codified in the timetable.

In the case of the daily 7:45 from nearby Kingham, the timetable is quite definitely in error, which explains why I was fortified with a home-cooked breakfast the first time I caught it. In search of the coach, I found myself in what appeared to be a dining car filled with passengers eating what looked like full breakfasts: toast and jam, bacon and eggs, hash-brown potatoes and grilled tomatoes.

Until I referred to the timetable again I suspected I had confused the crossed knife and fork symbol meaning restaurant with the teacup symbol meaning drinks and cold snacks only. But I hadn't. There it was in black and white, 0745, Monday through Friday, Kingham to Paddington, London, teacup, clear as a bell. I found an empty seat and decided another breakfast wouldn't do any harm.

"There must be some mistake here," I said to a spare old Englishman in rumpled tweeds across the table from me. "The timetable lists cold snacks for this train."

"Yes, but mercifully that isn't true," he smiled. "It's a long story."

As my companion explained it over a platter of kippered herring and scrambled eggs, an acute shortage of licensed chefs three years before had forced British Rails to eliminate the restaurant service on the 7:45 without eliminating the restaurant car, which remained hooked to the train while minor bureaucrats shuffled papers in an effort to replace it with the smaller cold-snack facilities. In the vacuum thus created, an employee who'd been working the car strictly as a waiter petitioned management to let him play chef, recruit his own staff, and keep the full service going. The fact that he's not yet a registered, fully certified chef accounts for the deceit. Officially, the 7:45 carries no restaurant— and officially I'm not eating those abundant hot breakfasts any time I go to London.

"Any idea what prompted the waiter to do it?" I asked.

"Ask him yourself," my table companion replied. "Bruce, chappie here wants a word with you."

Bruce listened politely.

"Well, now, we couldn't have these gentlemen ride into the city to business every day nothing but a cold sausage roll in them, could we?" he said.

Despite its reputation for inclement weather, England was so sunny our first summer that I actually managed to lay on a becoming Fire Island-type tan sitting in a deck chair out in the back garden when I should have been working. It was warm without being humid, in the seventies and low eighties, ideal weather for the occasional dip in the regular baby-sitter's pool three miles away. As our pediatrician back in New York used to tell us, baby-sitters should be chosen with great care.

The novel weather conditions, which one old-timer compared to the summer of 1936, seemed to catch everyone by surprise. Our chemist in Bourton, an enterprising merchant whose inventory bulges with umbrellas, plastic raincoats, and booties, hadn't allowed for the long run of sunshine burning a hole in the sky.

"And a bottle of suntan lotion, please," I said one morning, in ticking off a list of required sundries.

"I'm sorry." He shook his head tolerantly: mad dogs and Americans. "We don't carry sun oils."

In midsummer we found the English day stretched an hour or so longer than the American version. It's generally still light enough to read by at 9:30, and dawn begins to warm the surrounding hills at around five in the morning. Before long we reinforced the lined drapes in our bedroom windows with the kind of blackout curtains our nocturnal writer friend Harriet always carries on weekend visits outside of New York City as emergency equipment, although we never stuff a towel under the crack in the bedroom door like she does.

Any apprehension we had about the resident winters eventually melted away too. Although it's often raw and windy, the weather never dropped to the five and ten above zero levels that

41

were such a fixture of my Midwestern heritage. We experienced a total of just one snowfall our first winter, a fairly light one at that, but enough for Scott to sculpt a snowman in a field behind the mill. It was not, however, enough for other seasonal sports, as the mother of an eight-year-old grumped.

"Bought *me* daughter a *sledge* four Christmases ago—and she still hasn't had a chance to run it," she said.

But a second successive dry summer was too much of a good thing. Like everyone else in the village, Joan began bucketing water out of the stream to wet our small patch of garden. The weather affected more than farmers whose harvests weren't all they ought to have been. Worse, far worse, it also affected fishermen, among them me. Low water and the lack of the normal sheeting rains in April and May diminished the annual spawning run of salmon up the River Wye in Wales on which I'd arranged a beat for the full season. Although a couple of double-weight old sinners leaped out of the water and thumbed their noses at me, five trips to the Wye produced nothing more than a bit of ego gratification, which, come to think of it, is probably as rare and satisfying as killing a salmon. On the shelf of a secondhand store in a rural Welsh village stood a fairly clean copy of a book I'd written several years before, priced at two pounds, 20 pence, or $5.50 U.S.

If England experienced less rain than usual during our sojourn, it wasn't the first time I'd found myself in geography where weather conditions weren't as advertised. Years before, I was actually pinned down several days in an Algerian camelstop named Colomb-Bechar when a lorry trip scheduled to roll south over the rim of the Sahara Desert was delayed because of—see what I mean?—rain.

Although it was hot and dry by local standards, the weather failed to slow down the spawning run of tourists and what the British call day-trippers. Into Lower Slaughter they came, troops of men, women, and children, despite threatening double yellow lines painted on the roads and the lack of a tea room, an inn, and even so much as a public convenience. In they came to picnic on the green, splash in the stream, and shoot color film of young Cyril in his new jumper standing on the footbridge.

The inbound traffic inevitably included a number of Americans who strolled the village and whose down-home accents touched an old chord. Several of these were friends who had come out to visit us. Single guests were assigned our own spare bed; larger parties were booked into nearby inns. Depending on the length of their stay, we drove them to antique shops, introduced them to pork pies and genuine fish-and-chips, showed them Upper Swell and the Roman villa at Chedworth. An occasional guest who shared my warp joined me for an evening on the stream or quarry I lease.

In season we also fell into the habit of leading guests past the cemetery, through the allotment gardens, and over a wire fence to the village cricket pitch where a woolly baseball fanatic from New York had the pleasure of watching bearded Allan Hathaway, who swings the most thunderous blade for the home side, score a walloping total of sixty-eight runs. Fortunately, Hathaway's son doesn't swing nearly as hard, or else our youngster wouldn't have been able to hammer one of young Hathaway's front teeth out for cause at a cost of nothing more than a bruised hand.

"Your boy shouldn't be getting in punch-ups like that," a pro-Hathaway chidingly remarked.

"Like grandfather, like grandson," I replied. Scott's grandfather the dentist was especially expert at extractions.

The weekend that two mobile relatives from the Midwest, in England on one of those wall-to-wall theater charters, came for a visit, we made some arrangements restricted to special guests. At a cost of one pound, 50 pence, or $3.75 U.S., we hired the Village Hall for a modest bash, basic canapés and cocktails, invited a few English people we thought they might enjoy, and had a pleasant, rambling evening of amiable talk. Two twelve-year-old friends of our son, to whom he'd been passing olives out through a front window, insisted on helping police up afterward for what they described as their Boy Scout good deeds, which both claimed to be long overdue on.

Tourists in general, and American tourists in particular, became relatively scarce after the raw winter sucked the colors out of the day that first year. A few people still came through Slaughter, off-season trippers from places like York and Leeds, but it wasn't the same. On the basis of the slim pickings to be had, the mill bakery, which sold the outlanders ice lollies, picture postals, and plastic souvenirs through the summer, shut down on Sunday.

But the fact that the supply of Americans dried up almost completely in the winter didn't mean there was nobody with whom we could exchange an encouraging word. A peppery girl from Columbus, Ohio, lives in Bourton, a pilot from Vermont in Little Rissington, a former editor of a former magazine name of *Look*, in Broadway, and London is filled to the chimney pots with backslid Yanks, several of them good friends.

The registration book at Lords of the Manor in Upper Slaughter produced an occasional off-season American, too, which came in handy during headline news events like the Superbowl and the fuel crisis, when I wanted some unvarnished background detail from home. During an especially complicated strike action by professional NFL football players I hopefully worked the hotel like some fictional expatriate Britisher—Charles Laughton in such a role comes to mind—combing the beach in Jidda or Dar-es-Salaam trying to wheedle a drink and perhaps the cricket scores from sympathetic countrymen ashore from a luxury steamship standing out in the bay.

Any time I wanted to talk with Americans in large numbers, I had only to visit the U.S. Air Force base at Upper Heyford, twenty-five miles away, where a squadron of fighter planes stood poised at the edge of the runway like a flock of vultures. With its dependent kids dribbling basketballs and driving Ford Mustangs, sucking root beer and unwrapping Mounds bars, Heyford is an accurate reflection of America in the English countryside. I never realized quite how accurate a reflection it was until I struck up an uncomfortable conversation with a black enlisted man wearing shades and a modified Afro coiffure.

"Nice duty here at Heyford?" I asked.

"No! Not on this base, it ain't. Just lots of racism and lots of work."

"Is there more racism than in civilian life at home?" I couldn't help but pose the question for the sake of perspective.

"You bet. You can't answer back here. If you do they put you on the street with a bad discharge."

So much for perspective. Moments later, two white sergeants scaled to the size of Southeast Conference defensive tackles walked past talking pure boll weevil. The black cocked his head at the sound, stiffened slightly, and gave me one of those contented see-what-I-mean looks.

Whatever they think of service life on the Air Force reservation at Heyford, however, and opinions vary considerably, both the blacks and whites I spoke with admit to enjoying the soft favors out beyond the front gate. The longer they stay, the more they enjoy the pace, the litter-free landscape, and the people they rub up against. I met only two servicemen closing in on retirement, one an upstate New Yorker, the other a small-town Michigan product, but both told me they planned to permanently settle in England with their American wives and children once their enlistment tours lapsed.

Air Force personnel who find the United Kingdom the same comfortable fit we quickly found it aren't as unique as they might seem. A friend in London sent me a clipping scissored out of the international edition of the *Herald Tribune* citing the registrar general's *Statistical Review* as the source for a figure that more people emigrated from the United States to England than went the other direction in 1973, 22,200 to 16,600, which is a fairly decisive score. Joan and I weren't quite the originals we thought we were.

Chapter 5

Once we finally settled in we found that English fixtures such as telephones and television, economics and medicine, stuffy manners and the games people play, weren't as confusing as we originally had been led to believe. But the people, the perplexing British people, some of them dotty even among old-timers accustomed to close-up eccentrics, took far more sorting out.

Two instances taken from within hailing distance of our stone cottage suggest exactly how disconcerting all these various types can be. Our next-door neighbor to the east is Cyril Williams, cheery and spindly, a product of the village school, storeman for a construction company, without a telephone or car, whose generous wife hangs a Bed and Breakfast sign in their front window for stray tourists in search of lodging for the night. A man named Milward dwells directly across the stream from us, Sir Anthony Milward, C.B.E., O.B.E., Rugby School and Cambridge, former chairman of BEA, board member of BOAC and other blue chip enterprises, whose hobbies are fishing, shooting, and walking.

The impact of those and other highly diversified fellow Slaughters wasn't lost on an advertising executive friend from New York City who stepped off the agency treadmill long enough to do three days with us shortly before Christmas the first year of our sabbatical. Strolling the village one evening, he was introduced to a truck driver, a cleaning lady, and a squire whose substantial holdings enable him to do nothing at all.

"Mother of God, princes and paupers happily living hip-by-jowl together," he said, with the flair for hyperbole that won him his senior vice-presidential spurs on Madison Avenue only months before. "Whoever said the rigid old class barriers hadn't come tumbling down in the you-kay? Whoever said it ought to be taken straight to court and sued for a packet for slander."

At first glance, our guest's analysis seems perfectly accurate. On a zoning basis the socioeconomic mix is far more democratic than in my hometown of Aurora, Illinois, where plutocrats who own and fill executive jobs in the factories that sustain the locals live in one section, along with attendant lawyers, doctors, dentists, and architects, and the workers who punch the time clocks in those same plants inhabit quite another. In Aurora, the distance between outer Garfield Avenue and Pigeon Hill can't be measured in miles alone.

But in Lower Slaughter no such obvious segregation exists except for a high-roller property developer who lives behind a formidable barricade of stone walls in a manor house complete with a Rolls-Royce and a staff of servants and grooms to look after twenty-four rooms and the livestock. Although some homes in Lower Slaughter are larger than others, of course, our own being among the smallest, they aren't grouped on a basis of size like suits of racked clothes in a ready-to-wear store.

At first glance, the individuals who live in these homes have a friendly, comfortable relationship with one another. Executives and laborers alike pull on Wellington boots, clump in the common stream, and participate in the annual drive to cut the weed growth; all kinds of people knock on doors collecting rummage

47

—"I wear my rummage," Sir Anthony cracked at a Village Hall Committee meeting once—for the church sale; women of dramatically different backgrounds and circumstances agreeably work booths together at civic fetes. On the cricket pitch the second G.P. in a four-doctor surgery risks his valuable hands playing wicket-keeper for the home side, and a lank butcher swings an especially productive bat, which reminds me. . . .

Well over a century ago, long before the sainted Dr. W. Grace was enshrined as cricket's equivalent of Babe Ruth, the bluenose hierarchy that ruled the game catalogued competitors as either Gentlemen or Players. According to the rigid original specifications, Gentlemen were proper English bloods of private means who didn't soil their hands stockbrokering, reading the law, or otherwise lowering themselves in the commercial world, whereas Players, although decent chaps, some of whom could bowl a blistering yorker, were those who did. Down through the years, evolving realities such as an alarming decline of the leisure class have modified those expressions to a point where Gentleman currently means someone in the professional or executive sphere, and a Player is someone apt to work more with his hands than his skull. Despite that devaluation, the expressions have a nice flavor to them. For lack of any better codification, then, it's Gentlemen and Players throughout this confessional, not in a pejorative sense, it ought to be stressed, but strictly as a means of separating the men from the boys in terms of income, formal education, sophistication, and other standard criteria.

Sugar, toilet tissue, tinned raspberries, and Gentlemen occasionally have been in short supply, but Lower Slaughter suffers no shortage of those last basic models. Joan and I have had the pleasure of seeing them close up through a series of teas, pub crawls, dinners, cocktail parties, and other diversions peculiar to each breed.

"The port, Deindorfer, the port. Please hand the port along. No, no, good God, not that way. Hand the port along clockwise, won't you, please."

Michael Downes lifted his voice just enough to be heard in Lower Swell, two miles away. Outgoing and red-faced, past master of both the fox and otter hounds, Downes is a Gentleman in the classic as well as the reformed sense. Perspiring a bit from the strain of a five-course dinner ingested not long before, our friend and neighbor sat at the head of the table under a magnificent oil of his great-great-grandmother, in a formal dining room all sputtering candlelight, oak paneling, red velvet, and oils. The women had been dismissed from the room in the ancient ritual, leaving the males with their cigars, their port, and their masculine dialogue, which was pleasant for me despite the social breach of inadvertently fanning a crystal carafe of port toward Downes in the wrong direction.

As the evening wore on, conversation veered from racing to fox hunts to beagling for hare, reinforced with enough bald Elizabethan English to awaken echoes of locker room talk back home. After the four of us started pecking away at a third carafe of the port, our large likable host leaned back in his period chair —dangerously far back, I thought to myself, for the sake of the chair if not for Downes—and got down to what could only be described as cases in a literal sense of the word.

"It's too young, too young," he said.

"What's that?" Drummond Angus hunched forward.

"The port, the bloody port. It's too young. It's at least a year away."

Sir Geoffrey, who'd had his pink nose in the stuff like the rest of us without a whimper of complaint, was quick to agree.

"Easily, Michael. It's too young."

"Still, it's a fairly decent port for its age, isn't it?" Downes lifted his glass. The carafe went round one last time. "I expect we'd better join the ladies now."

If I'd had far more than my normal quota by the time we moved into the lounge to reclaim our wives—in the dizzy wine-engendered haze of the evening it appeared for a while to be Sir Geoffrey's wife I was trying to reclaim—I could hardly be blamed. After all, the scene was straight out of the films, the radio dramas, the books I'd fed on as a boy in Aurora.

Fortunately, I had packed a dinner jacket along to England on the off chance the Flyfishers of London, the English-Speaking Union, the Press Association, or some other fraternal lodge extending me reciprocal privileges might schedule the occasional black tie bash in trendy swinging London. Over the years my size 45 extra-long jacket has absorbed its share of cigar ash, port, and, as a practicing bachelor for many years in New York City, an occasional whisper of lipstick up along the shoulder as well, but I hadn't ever guessed it would enjoy its first official British outing in our remote village.

Not long after that experience a female Player Joan and I are very fond of thoughtfully invited us to join her for an evening of gaming at the British Legion in Bourton. She suggested we arrive a bit ahead of the scheduled eight o'clock starting time, a wise precaution, we found, since other Players afflicted with the same fever soon filled most of the folding chairs. I couldn't help but compare the total attendance of 298 males and females, many of whom I'd seen and talked with over the counters at the greengrocer's, snack bars, and ironmonger's, with a congregation of exactly 17, almost all of them Gentlemen, for what it's worth, at the 11 o'clock service at St. Mary's Anglican Church in Slaughter the previous Sunday. But these Players were good, decent people; and who was to begrudge them another evening of shiny hopes after brewing pots of tea, wrapping cabbages, and pumping petrol for others all day long?

Ballpoint pens or freshly sharpened pencils poised, two and sometimes even three cards spread out before them, they anxiously awaited the semiweekly ritual. Eventually a man with a surprising tinny voice stepped forward to spin the box and pull the first number. "Twenty-six," he called. Souls more fortunate than I crossed out the magic number on their cards. One after the other he called numbers with an occasional flutter of familiar by-play.

It wasn't long before a fat lady who'd sold me a platter of eggs and chips at the milk bar earlier in the day triumphantly shouted "bingo" a few rows in front of us. The wind audibly went out of several fellow Players who'd been within a single number of the eight pounds, or $20 U.S., bonanza themselves. Within less than an hour the competition finished, and part of the crowd relocated in the British Legion lounge to visit, order drinks, and play two fruit machines, as the English call the highly toxic one-armed bandits, as a means of tapering off slowly without attempting a cold-turkey cure. We were home by ten—in contrast to Downes's dinner party, which had lasted until two in the morning—and we meant every word of it when we thanked our hostess for an illuminating and enjoyable evening.

But any outlander's assumption that these Gentlemen and Players who share the same rural village fraternize on a social level is illusion. They don't. They nod, chat with one another, and enjoy what seems a respectful two-sided relationship without ever quite breaching subtle class lines such as dinner parties or trips to the theater in Stratford. A Gentleman we like very much who's lived in Slaughter for eight years has yet to set foot inside the home of a Player two doors away—and vice versa, of course—although, to the Gentleman's credit, he has gotten as far as the Player's doorway to drop off a gift brace of trout he'd lifted out of his own private waters.

Specific examples of the social stratification include the use of the word "Mister," which Players invariably use for Gentlemen, even when their names happen to arise in Players' private conversations. One evening a lifelong Player treated me to a bewildering sample of this by persisting in prefacing the name of a Gentleman he was discussing in scalding personal terms with the standard Mister, even when his spleen was venting fairly hard. On the other hand, Gentlemen refer to Players without a preliminary Mister and often use only their surnames: Howse, Shaw, Dixon.

Both groups work together on various committees that keep

the village spinning, but their roles within the civic structure are quite different. Although Players who serve as members of the Parish Council and the Village Hall Committee sell as many— and often more—tickets for the annual fund-raising raffles and such than Gentlemen, it's inconceivable that one would ever be tapped as chairman, vice-chairman, or secretary-treasurer of the committees. Consequently, the executive positions rotate among the resident supply of Gentlemen in a continuing game of musical chairs, with an occasional female Gentleman even put up for office. On asking a Gentleman why this was so, I learned the facts of life. "They're very nice chaps, you know, reliable, hard-working, but they have no experience at this sort of thing," he replied. And I see no signs that the first requirement of on-the-job training is about to commence, either.

Undoubtedly, the most dramatic instance of the separate but equal stratification unfolds during the Christmas season, when Gentlemen and Players stroll the village behind a doctor with a clarinet, all of them singing seasonal carols. On a frosty night of our first Christmas we participated, the carolers lifted their voices outside a total of six homes, into three of which we were invited for mulled wine, with cookies and orange squash for musicians whose voices had yet to change. Every one of the six homes caroled to belonged to a Gentleman.

One thing that brings deep yet hidden differences boiling to the surface is the matter of trippers, day-trippers, and weekend tourists, most of them English, who fill up the village during summer months. Almost without exception Gentlemen would like to discourage the inflow, whereas Players like A. C. Collett, whose mill bakery sells postals, souvenirs, and ice lollies as well as five-star oven-fresh bread, take a more sympathetic view for reasons of their own. One notable exception is the female Gentleman whose engaging warp—several seasons before she had whimsically suggested that the footbridge be greased so trippers would fall into the stream—relaxed considerably once she began doing a selective Bed and Breakfast business herself.

The controversy reached a noisy climax at an especially contentious parish meeting in the Village Hall a few weeks after we had arrived as something more than trippers. In general the Gentlemen wanted more double yellow lines painted on the local roadways, and the Players fewer. In the end a compromise was effected by voting the status quo—and cars, caravans, and even what my father used to call damned rubberneck buses continued to pile into our village to sightsee over the weekends.

In a way, that fundamental division illustrates the changing character of Slaughter and, for all I know, other attractive villages scattered through rural England. Many younger Players move from the village to get closer to their jobs with construction firms, motor works, or industrial estates. In come the Gentlemen, many of them retired or close to it, lawyers, educators, and businessmen in search of a bosky dell retreat after years of stacking it up in metropolitan areas. They really can't be blamed for wanting to keep trippers off their front gardens any more than Players born and raised right in the village can be blamed for wanting to watch the cars go by, especially if a few of them pause long enough to buy a coronet of ice cream or a few imperial gallons of petrol or to sign on for a night's lodging.

Although an otherwise affable and harmless Player who lives not far from us can hardly be described as a traitor to his class, his personal view of trippers doesn't fit into the normal groove. He has gone so far as to deflate a tire on the car of some visitor imprudent and/or innocent enough to park in the spot on the village green he has come to consider his own for reasons of common law. One dark night when he returned from the Coach and Horses to find his space preempted by a newcomer to Slaughter, he deflated not one but all four tires on the reasonable grounds that, the culprit being an actual resident, she ought to know better.

Our neighbor's prickly reluctance to forgive those that trespass against his private carpark isn't sufficient to qualify him as one of the reigning characters. Although Slaughter can't lay claim to any resident characters as bizarre as the twenty-seven-year-old Yorkshire man who legally changed his name to Elvis Presley or the wacky prizefight buff who actually named his daughter after every last one of the world's former heavyweight champions, in proper sequence—Maria Sullivan Corbett Fitzsimmons Jeffries Hart Burns Johnson Willard Dempsey Tunney Schmeling Sharkey Carnera Baer Braddock Louis Charles Walcott Marciano Patterson Johansson Liston Clay Frazier Foreman Brown, to spin out a full monicker for which she ought to file a damage action against her father—we do have several stock figures entitled to some mention. They include the kind bulky man so obsessed with his kitchen garden that a lifelong friend said he expects to see him watering it during a sheeting rain; a monosyllabic blank-faced Player closing in on retirement who strips off everything except his tattered cap for what he mistakenly seems to think is a secret plunge in a cow tank or the River Eye where it washes through a field beyond the public footpath; a meddlesome, accident-prone hysteric—she'd make a local town crier redundant—who managed to skewer the good names of three Gentlemen and two Players during a brief encounter one evening.

My own favorite off-beat type is an attractive fifteen-year-old Huck Finn who mastered the art of poaching to a point where he was able to clean the stocked rainbow trout out of a pond at Lords of the Manor in Upper Slaughter without getting caught. With cover identity as essential to successful poachers as it is to espionage agents, who have rather different fish to fry, Quentin seems a natural. His smile is so winning, his manner so respectful, his speech so appealing, and his baggy look so innocent that only the most cynical protective riverkeeper would ever ask him if those spotted silvery things didn't happen to be trout.

The sight of Quentin walking a heavy nine-foot fiberglass rod, a can of worms, and an empty plastic bucket past our cottage in the morning and then returning late in the afternoon with an empty can and a bucket filled to the scuppers with fresh-caught trout soon became as fixed as neighbors toddling out to work their gardens late each afternoon. As Quentin told me in bashful detail, he later walked the bucket into Bourton and peddled the bootleg fish out behind cafés and hotels.

Technically an outsider from London who comes to visit his grandmother for the summer holiday, the young poacher seems happy in a rural environment he can turn to such material advantage. His face actually glistened with pleasure the night he told me his parents had phoned to say he could stretch his holiday in Slaughter for two more weeks. "I don't know if the local trout can put up with me for another fortnight," he said, in a voice that clearly indicated they couldn't.

The last time I saw Quentin before he finally did pack off to London he was smiling that special smile and standing behind a table he'd erected in front of his grandmother's house wholesaling fresh-picked plums at what a rude lettered sign priced at 10 pence the bag. Although I probably should have known better, I was so impressed with this demonstration of free-enterprise clean living in view of his poaching that I congratulated him and bought a sack of what he assured me were the pick of his grandmother's trees.

In a conversation with one of the local youngsters who had also come to know Quentin, I remarked that it was nice he'd been able to earn a little pocket money picking and marketing plums from his grandmother's orchard. "Oh, his granny *don't* have any plum trees," the child said, fixing me with a stricken look.

If the supply of characters is sufficient, the supply of headline celebrities is nonexistent. In a tenuous way Lower Slaughter vaguely claims two theatrical figures, Wilfrid Hyde-White, the actor, who was born and raised in Bourton, his father the vicar whose circuit-riding ministry included the satellite church in Slaughter, and Susannah York, the actress, who lived several years of her youth in the enormous manor house in Upper Slaughter. According to several sources who insist there's no mistake about it, John Milton wrote part of "Paradise Lost" in a stone cottage just over a roll of hills to the north of Slaughter, too.

The closest thing we have to an authentic resident celebrity is Cynthia Hayden, a bouncy, unaffected lady who drives, trains, shows, and otherwise dominates the English hackney horse scene. The fact that her picture often appears in national newspapers and on television, combined with her downhome manner, helped diminish some testy objections raised at the time she and her husband first bought a big local property to stable themselves, their staff, and their high-stepping horses.

Nobility doesn't really count as headline material, at least not any more it doesn't, else an angular old citizen Joan and I encountered outside an iron gate adorned with a large heraldic ancestor-drop in six living colors in Bourton might be included. Behind the gate a gravel drive rolled up to a huge pile of a building I'd been wondering about.

"Is this some sort of a hospital, a rest home, or institution?" I inquired of the old boy.

A wry smile eased the lines in his rusty face. "Yes, yes, in a way it is, don't you know. This is a home for elderly people, two elderly people, my wife and myself."

On reporting our discovery to the tire-deflating maniac back in Slaughter later, we collected additional detail. "Lord Buchan, that's who it was, rich bloke too; we used to queue up there every Christmas when I was a toddler for a penny and a bun," he said.

Lower Slaughter does have what I consider a disproportionately large number of residents of some accomplishment. In addition to Michael Downes, Sir Anthony, the Haydens, and that high-roller property developer whose product is said to be ruining the Spanish landscape, the ranks of the Gentlemen also consist of two doctors, two architects, three retired business executives, a lawyer, three teachers, a breeder of blue-ribbon show dogs, and a building mogul whose payroll numbers more than fifty employees drawn from miles around.

The population, while smaller by actual count than the apartment building on the corner of Park Avenue and Seventy-first Street just up the block from us back in New York City, is so eclectic, in fact, that there's nothing really to distinguish us, although originally I had assumed—assumed, not hoped—we couldn't help but stand out in a diminutive rural hamlet. We're not even the only Americans dwelling in Lower Slaughter. A young Pennsylvania girl with a heartbreak of a face is also here learning the hackney horse business.

As for my modest credentials as a writer, again I was taking too much for granted, as Joan let me know while a weekend guest from Manhattan and I enacted a silly interview vaudeville after leaning on too much malt late one night.

"And who would you say is the most prominent, most widely published author in all of Lower Slaughter, suburban as well as downtown Lower Slaughter, Mr. Deindorfer?" he asked, holding a phantom microphone to my face.

"Modesty really prohibits me from answering. . . ."

"Modesty—and Doctor Smith," Joan said.

When she explained her breach of good manners, our friend's playful query turned out to be not nearly as rhetorical as he and I assumed. Although it was the first I'd known about it, Dr. T. Smith, Gentleman, neighbor and fellow communicant at church, was also Dr. T. Smith, Oxford don, former visiting professor at both Princeton and the University of Pennsylvania, special consultant to the UN, and distinguished demographer with a total of eight books to his credit—all of which suggests there's probably no village small enough for me to be the chief writer in residence, no matter how several Gentlemen and Players tend to exaggerate my literary rating.

Chapter 6

Until we finally chose to settle in England I had always contributed more than my proper quota to the lower depths. The mean experience of having my pockets picked during a brief visit to Basra in Iraq was unique only in the sense that I hadn't ever been victimized in the Persian Gulf before. But over a period of all too many years I have been burgled in places as diverse as Columbia, Missouri; Vaduz, Liechtenstein; Stony Brook, Long Island; Timbuktu, West Africa; and, along with everyone else, New York City, where knaves cleaned me out on five separate occasions without the law so much as once—to use their own lyrics—"apprehending the perpetrator." The fact that I haven't yet been hit at the office is undoubtedly because I've been giving so regularly at home.

In especially lugubrious moments, which seem to close in on me with some frequency lately, I suspect that if it's my good fortune to eventually qualify for the Kingdom of Heaven, I'll probably get mugged a few yards short of the Pearly Gates.

In view of my chronic role as the easiest mark in the neighborhood, any neighborhood at all, I couldn't help but be pleasantly warmed by my first encounter with English morality back in 1959, or long before we alighted for an extended period in that country. The wear and tear of a long visit in London was such that my father, whose memory was beginning to fuzz a bit, anyway, climbed out of a taxi without remembering to retrieve his camera, which he and I were counting on to officially notarize for friends back home some epic trout we hoped to kill in Scotland the next week.

"Damnation!" My father's dismay was audible as the taxi tailed up the street, around a corner, and out of sight. "Twenty-four rolls of fresh film in my bag—and now no camera. Damnation!"

As Americans, lifelong Americans, my father and I couldn't be blamed for writing the camera off and wondering about the cost of replacing it. Neither of us would have considered reporting the loss if a London bobby hadn't come by while we stood there cursing our fate. Sadly, sadly, we outlined the full details.

"No problem, sir," the constable said, scratching on a pad. "You can pick up the camera at Lost and Found at this address at nine tomorrow morning. Good day."

As things turned out, the camera actually was there at Lost and Found, near Lambeth Castle, next morning. My father redeemed it by contributing one-tenth of its official list price, or far less than a licensed pawnbroker would have paid the taxi driver if he'd reacted like many other drivers elsewhere, including the one who drove away with my $200 eight-by-sixty Leitz binoculars in New York City several years later. What impressed me most of all, however, was the blunt fact that, besides the police officer, three other English people—the porter at our hotel and a couple we had dinner with—assured us beyond any doubt that the camera would indeed be turned in to Lost and Found.

In case I hadn't dropped in on England fairly regularly following that awakening experience, I might have counted it the exception rather than the rule. But I have come to learn that Old

59

Blighty is fairly unique in the matter of law and order. On one subsequent trip, for example, I sailed on the *Queen Mary*, a great joy, especially when I discovered that virtually nobody bothered locking their cabin door, although I did, or at least I did the moment I realized that my fellow passengers not only weren't exclusively English but included an alarming smattering of Americans. The man who made up my cabin expressed genuine surprise when I told him I wanted a key to lock up every time I aimed for the dining room for another boiled dinner.

On other vacation trips to England I found that open-door policy was almost routine outside of London. At inns and hotels situated in Oxford and Seaton, Harrogate and Kendall, occupants up and down the hallway did something more than leave their shoes outside the doors for a charity polish without any fears they'd walk away during the night. They also seldom bothered with the big brass keys hung up on the board behind the front desk.

Eventually I even managed to discover exactly what it was about London that seemed especially spooky. Even after allowing for the left-hand traffic pattern, the nasal accents, the leisurely pace, and the indigenous cooking odors, London is different from New York City in some baffling special way I couldn't quite get a grip on until the night I nearly leaped out of a comfortable bed in a Kensington hotel filled with a wild sense of I've-got-it. After too many years in New York City the everlasting sound of a round-the-clock police siren wailing somewhere close by both day and night had become so commonplace that my eardrums automatically filtered the noise right out. In London the two-beat sound of the police siren is wonderfully rare.

In talks with English friends, resident journalists, and an occasional bobby walking his beat I've confirmed the accuracy of that deafening silence. There is simply far less crime in every category from murder right down to breaching the traffic regulations, except, of course, for poaching. In a country where most of the good fishing water belongs to the Gentlemen, the Players who dream either of catching or of dining off a fresh trout or salmon have no choice other than ignoring all the Private Water —No Trespassing signs. But anglers elsewhere, up to and specifically including this one, generally show a dim sense of property rights, anyway.

With the supply of criminals obviously short of the artistic demand, off-shore lower-order types can't be blamed for shuttling into England from the Continent any time the pickings look especially ripe. According to Scotland Yard, inbound traffic picks up during the Ascot races, international cricket test matches, and the peak of the summer tourist season. On the day of Princess Anne's Royal Wedding, seven pickpockets from Italy, three from France, and two from Spain—garment workers, in police vernacular—who flew in strictly for the festivities were arrested as they fanned the huge crowds gathered in the Mall and Whitehall. And five artful craftsmen who'd traveled all the way from Yugoslavia for the English soccer championships got caught just as they began warming up outside Wembley Stadium.

Exactly why crime rates throughout England are so low by American standards is a matter I best leave to more qualified sociologists. But I have heard a number of explanations that strike me as being reasonable: the population mix isn't excessive; England happens to be a tight little island and the family unit, although gradually becoming more fragmented, provides a discipline base; bobbies walk a particular beat long enough to learn a neighborhood and its occupants; the English are more orderly by their very nature; and things like handguns are almost impossible to come by.

"Why do you Yanks commit so many more murders than our chaps?" A young bobby sitting in a patrol car parked outside a London discotheque got to brooding on my query early one morning. "I expect the main difference is that you don't have any gun-control laws, do you?"

Whether his explanation happens to fit or not, the difference in gun-control laws is decisive. Despite some recent legislation in

America, it's still possible to order guns by mail and buy cheap Saturday Night Specials in some sporting goods shops. On the other hand, it's almost impossible for the average Englishman to acquire a handgun, much less carry it around, and, as everyone knows, even police assigned to preserving law and order manage without firearms.

In the view of many English law-enforcement people, any lapse in the rigid British gun-control laws would put weapons of death in the hands of both latent and actual criminal types and the police, which inevitably might lead to the nightmare image Robert Oppenheimer developed in a different context: "Two scorpions in a bottle." Not even weapons-oriented English outdoorsmen who maintain a legal rack of sports rifles and shotguns object to the rigid controls on handguns, which, while already severe, are further tightened every so often. There's no denying the fact that some 10,000—that's right, 10,000—Americans are shot to death every year.

In searching for the key to upright British morality the formidable efficiency of the professionals engaged in law-enforcement work ought not to be overlooked. In areas as small as Chipping Camden and as enormous as London the constable is a man to be reckoned with. Tough, patient, and aware, he is so tuned in to the specific beat he walks that he may occasionally distribute small gifts to resident children on their birthdays. If the constable is challenged, he's not above showing the required muscle, although he'd much prefer to write out a ticket or walk the offender down to the station house instead.

An enterprising police constable in Oxford, whose academic population numbers students from more than seventy different countries, enjoyed a brief celebrity several years ago by making the punishment neatly fit the crime. After uncovering a roomful of university pranksters who'd poached an old man's bicycle as a lark, he took matters into his own hands by ordering them to do time cleaning, sweeping, and gardening at an old folks' home rather than being officially booked for the crime they'd committed.

Hard-line law-and-order Americans constantly demand stricter law enforcement, but this demand is missing in England. It might be a coincidence, nothing more, although I doubt it, but the whole apparatus is surprisingly lenient by our standards. Americans who belong to the Silent Majority clamor for more night sticks, more prison sentences, and more capital punishment to bring down the growing crime rate, but the stress is far different from Land's End to York. The English not only have no capital punishment but constables seldom play tunes on suspect's skulls with the night stick, and in England ten years amounts to a very long prison sentence.

Along with these and other relatively lenient practices, the prison structures themselves would seem odd to Love It Or Leave It Americans who keep asking for higher walls, stiffer security, and more discipline on the inside. Like it or not, the walls of British prisons are soft as pudding, as a number of transient tenants—Blake, The Great Train Robbers, Donnell— happily discovered. Other than a mild flutter of letters to the editor, no great hullaballoo developed following the frequent escapes.

Law-enforcement people in England manage to resolve a far greater percentage of both trivial and serious crimes than do comparable American officials. Whizbang efficiency right through the system is so brisk that suspects are caught, booked, brought to trial, and either sentenced or set free within three months of the crime, or about the time it takes a New York cop to fill out in triplicate those forms some other cop spilled coffee over several weeks before.

In terms of numbers, crime levels in England and America show a walloping big difference. I audited figures for New York City and London for the full calendar year of 1972 just before we arrived in England to live on the reasonable grounds that both of those two great urban sprawls number more than 8 million people. Admittedly, 1972 was an especially vexing year for New York police. But aren't they all? One hot July night, residents did one another in to the tune of thirteen homicides, and the total for a full week in July of that same year came to fifty-eight. Still, the annual homicide rate was about what authorities expected, which illustrates how very bleak our expectations have become.

Even with the London figures rising some while the New York City total remained fairly static, the comparative totals for 1972 show why Londoners feel perfectly safe walking their cobbled streets day and night.

	London	New York City
Assault	7,859	31,128
Forcible Rape	135	3,271
Robbery	3,168	78,204
Murder	113	1,690

Some numbers, eh, sports fans? The fact that New York City ranked far down the U.S. scale—for instance, eighth in murders per capita, fourth in overall crime per capita—only makes the bulge more depressing. And anyone who suspects that London might be especially safe even by proper British standards need merely consider the national totals. America, with four times the population of England and Wales, had 18,300 murders in 1972, or more than 120 times as many as the modest 149 scrags in the United Kingdom, which Anglophobes undoubtedly will mark up to a lack of get-up-and-go in the British lower depths.

"Godalmighty, only 149 murders in England last season," a visiting friend from Georgia remarked after studying the annual harvest figures. "Why, we had 255 right in Atlanta."

My friend's arithmetic can't be faulted. Neither can the assembly-line casualty figures from friendly old Motown Detroit: 751 murders for 1973, with a high of 76 in September.

Predictably, the low English crime rates prevail out in the Cotswolds area we inhabit, too. In the first few weeks of our occupancy I was hitting the conversational high spots with a neighbor who, if he isn't the reigning local authority on virtually everything, at least doesn't mind if I mistake him for same. After some preliminary nattering, I asked him about burglaries in our small community.

"Oh, I can't recall a one," he said. "But there was a robbery last summer—or was it the summer before last?—over in Stow. Someone stole a side of beef from out behind a butcher shop."

An exaggeration? Not at all. On checking with the police in Bourton-on-the-Water, whose jurisdiction includes Lower Slaughter, I learned that the crime sheets for our village have remained blank for nine golden years, aside from transgressors who breach speed and traffic laws or park on the forbidden double yellow lines. At the time I spoke with them the police seemed in a professional lather at not having caught up with the anonymous jock who frequently rides a rackety motorcycle through Lower Slaughter late at night.

The tidy state of British virtue is widely applauded by everyone, of course, but it does pose something of a circulation problem for newspaper people. In England, as elsewhere, editors can't be blamed for wanting to liven up front pages gone gray with economic forecasts and inflation spiral reports with the splashy colors of a suspenseful murder, a big number bank robbery, or a splendid society rape. With police blotters offering such slim pickings, however, they are forced to make do with what they have, which sometimes means another one of those football pool stories about 50,000 pounds sterling going to some winner so old he doesn't have any remaining teeth to enjoy the money with, which are regularly treated as Stop Press news. Consequently, the English are treated to front-page crime headlines—Vandals Loot Country Home, Man Admits Receiving Stolen Two Pounds, Fine Youth Who Lived In Car—so bland they wouldn't be ventilated even in small American weeklies.

On a purely professional level, a transplanted resident from New York City, where the papers practically run a daily body count of homicides, can't help but pity English journalists assigned to pump some juice into modest infractions of the moral code. Among all too many other front-page instances, the long and inflamed account of a seventeen-year-old boy who was fined ten pounds for stealing an umbrella in a hotel lobby on a wet night struck me as wonderfully resourceful. Exhibit A ("a white golfing umbrella"), the exact time it disappeared ("half after nine at night"), the identity of the constable ("Inspector C. Bowler") who solved the case so quickly, and the recovery site ("the back garden of a house in Cornish Road, Chipping Norton") were pumped to compelling dimensions.

Under all the circumstances, personally we can't help but feel wonderfully safe in Lower Slaughter without the three locks and the iron bar behind which we fortified ourselves back in New York City. In point of fact, we generally leave either the front or the back door, and often both, unlocked while we're out—and I have yet to turn a key in the door of our car.

Yet the fact that Lower Slaughter has absolutely no resident crime doesn't necessarily mean that it has no resident criminal. It has. Our sparse population includes a stalwart member of the Parish Council and the village cricket team who breached the law to a point where he was eventually arrested, tried and sentenced to three years as an accessory in 9,000 pounds sterling worth of burglaries several miles away. In lifting an occasional pint with him before he was picked up by the police, I found this neighbor a warm, witty, and immensely likable man who happened to share my own appreciation of Jaguar XJ motorcars.

News of any sort involving local residents being rare, a story of his arrest in the daily *Gloucester Echo* fed village small talk for several days, with the people dividing into two factions: innocent and guilty, good and bad. The division did not seem to reflect the existing socioeconomic stratification, although I got the impression the resident Gentlemen were rather more tolerant than his own fellow Players.

"Oh, he was corrupted by bad company he kept," one Gentleman suggested.

"Lazy, he's always been a bit lazy," a female Player countered.

Every so often the disagreement among friends and neighbors rose to a point of genuine rancor. In one instance an overbearing female intruded in an effort to effect a peaceful compromise, which was admirable, of course, if only she'd got the basic facts straight.

"You have to remember he got caught up in the austerity three-day work week," she said, a strident lack of logic to start with, like the old joke now we know you're a whore and the only question is the going rate. As the newspaper story had pointed out, the burglaries unfolded in 1971, or two years before the energy crunch and coal miners' strike produced the three-day week.

Any suspicions that our lapsed neighbor might look on the rest of us as fairly easy pickings while he was out on bail—especially with his legal expenses—failed to produce a run on the closest locksmith two miles away. Most people maintained the standard open-door policy on the grounds that the resident burglar wouldn't think of patronizing local homes.

"Even if he's guilty he'd not break into *me* cottage," an audible Player commented during an informal group discussion on the footbridge early one evening. "Why, we've known one another a donkey's years."

For hazy reasons that defy analysis I shared that same reassuring view. During a long visit before they put him away, my burglar friend and I talked the familiar old subjects. Neither of us offered up a word about his big problem, but I was tempted to suggest that, judges being what they are, this did not strike me as the ideal moment for him to start raising a beard. There'd be time enough for that later—three years, minus a few months off for good behavior later, as things turned out.

A droll London friend without the foggiest notion that we

enjoy and sometimes fraternize with our certified local burglar —if and when he's at liberty, that is—couldn't resist a characteristic impulse on reading a lurid Village Sports Star Was a Thief at Night rehash story in the national *Daily Mail.* He scissored it out, added a peckish marginal comment—"I hear they're after the Mr. Big in this operation, which explains why you've gone to ground"—and mailed it off to me.

The glossy level of morality we have grown accustomed to in England even rubs off on Scott, who can't help but tune in to the occasional conversation about our giddy prospects of making it through the day without being mugged. Back in New York City, watching local television newscasts had made him all too aware of the potluck risks and the tally of street crimes.

Through some childish lurch of logic Scott also managed to relate the beneficial law and order in England with the Toy Fairy, a convenient fiction we had concocted, who stops by regularly every night to recover any playthings our son hasn't properly filed away before he grudgingly packs off to bed.

"Maybe they don't have a Toy Fairy here who comes and nicks a kid's cars," he hopefully suggested once after Joan and I had discussed the astonishing English crime figures.

In just over a year in England this lifelong pigeon has been done in a total of exactly once, but even that breach can't be counted. Returning to the car one afternoon I went into a memorable rage on finding that a pack of cigarettes and a fresh copy of *Time* magazine—gold, pure gold, especially with me trying to sort out both the Watergate hearings and the major league pennant races unfolding three thousand frustrating miles away—had disappeared from the front seat where I'd left them.

Since the car was parked inside a U.S. Air Force base at Upper Heyford, the rustler obviously had an accent as alien to the British Midlands as my own. Now that I can see the incident in its proper focus—you know, buggered again, probably for old time's sake, by a fellow countryman, who else—I'm surprised I became so wrathful. Frankly, I'm surprised I didn't get gooey homesick all over being the typecast patsy once again.

Chapter 7

During a series of impromptu background briefings before we packed off from New York City a writer friend who had done a pleasant hitch in England provided a list of native deadfalls to be approached with extreme caution—if they had to be approached at all. Along with such fixtures as lawn bowling, pork pies, and what pass for martinis, the roll specifically included the English Gentleman, about whom our friend nourished some stiff incidental reservations despite a generally favorable view.

"There's far more to the gent than the old tintype suggests," our knowledgeable source remarked. "He's informed, witty, generous, surprisingly tolerant, and fair-minded." But the classic English gentleman is also a four-point bellyacher who forever sees the world about to go bang.

As the writer described them, those stock upper-class characters thunder against the prevailing status quo regardless of the realities. In good times as well as bad they grump over their port and cigars, railing about trade unions and politicians, flabby British spirit and the ruins of an empire. They are jubilant doomsayers who almost achieve a point of sexual gratification enumerating the many troubles, real and imagined, that beset them. On settling in Lower Slaughter we quickly found that our friend hadn't been exaggerating by much. The condition was even more pronounced, in fact, because the chronic English scolds never had it so good. The parlous state of practically everything in England, which, except for our own life style, was idyllic for all the forbidding headlines, made it a vintage period for the bellyachers. They promptly took to howling at the moon with a perverse new gusto, as, for once at least, they had legitimate reasons to.

We arrived in the midst of an inflationary spiral that has yet to turn around and that everyone quite properly laments. Prices have been rising at a slower rate than those back in America and in several other countries, but the gloomy trend was a particular problem for consumers locked in the sterling economy. Sterling itself was off in relation to the dollar, tailing to a historic low around Christmas of our first year in England, a pleasure for me and our convertible dollars, if not for the locals. Meanwhile, England's sizzling balance of payments gap went up, up, up like an economic boil.

If price levels and trade deficits went up, an ailing stock market most certainly didn't. As bulb-nosed old J. P. charitably disclosed to the American people, the market will continue to fluctuate, only it fluctuated mostly downward in England, until share prices hit a fifteen-year low by the end of our first full season. Those English gentlemen with their birthrights invested in ICI, Whitbread, or Peacock Sasini whimpered louder than ever.

The troubles in Northern Ireland persisted, heartbreaking, beyond any visible solution. Soldiers were shot; men, women and children were blown to bits; it was a tragedy so constant it no longer even qualified as front-page news unless IRA provisional warriors planted bombs in Manchester, London's Paddington Station, or the Tower of London. On three separate occasions the

London airport was ringed with soldiers on full alert, a bristling show of force in case Irish or Arab guerillas, or both, actually planned to do in a few airplanes.

As an American born into an age when the U.S. trade union movement was having almost as negative an effect on the economy as the National Association of Manufacturers traditionally had, labor strikes are old stuff to me, but what began happening in England stretched my tolerance to the breaking point. One after the other various trade unions threatened or embarked on strike actions—railway drivers, nurses, mechanical engineers, journalists, printers, television technicians, dock wallopers, X-ray people, motorcycle and auto workers, a Who's Who of the bib overall set.

"Well, should we watch the trade union news tonight?" Joan asked one evening during an especially tiresome run of labor unrest. In those circumstances we frequently dialed in the self-serving Voice of America radio news programs instead.

Far and away the gravest blow came when the coal miners, whose spokesmen had been making the usual angry noises, finally abandoned their shovels in a full-blown strike. As they knew only too well, the revolt couldn't have come at a worse time. In a vengeful, perfectly understandable aftermath to the war in the Middle East a few months earlier in the autumn of 1973, all those Arab states Allah in His infinite wisdom had situated on top of half the world's known oil reserves seriously restricted the flow and then stepped it back to normal again only after jacking prices so high that for a while it was difficult to buy a good secondhand bicycle in the Cotswolds.

Whipsawed by events plainly out of control, uncertain exactly which of the many adversities should be given priority, the government waffled some before taking the usual prudent steps. Petrol stations were shut down on Sundays, a national speed limit of 50 mph was announced, and motorists queued up at post offices for ration books Her Majesty's Government had run off just in case. Although the ration books obviously have no current market value, I laid mine away as a future collector's item, like a few NRA seals I accumulated in my youth.

As more serious, more dismaying troubles unfolded, England even suffered diplomatic humiliations at the hands of sovereign powers of no loftier rank than Iceland and Uganda, which undoubtedly felt they might just as well take their turn tweaking the tail of the ailing British Lion. The Concorde supersonic aircraft built on a joint-venture basis with the French successfully passed its flight tests, but potential sales looked discouraging, if not downright disastrous, and a costly new nuclear reactor unit expected to sell like hotcakes and give lift to British economy didn't.

"Good Lord, what next?" Joan said as she skimmed the local papers one night.

"Turn to the sports section for full details," I suggested.

In the midst of its other manifold miseries an especially shameful defeat occurred when England, which literally had invented the game of soccer, failed to qualify for the final rounds of the World Cup, prompting a torrent of outraged letters to the editor, elaborate postmortems on what went wrong—an overemphasis on defensive soccer, many authorities decided—and, inevitably, a change in management, with a head coach who'd been knighted following England's World Cup title eight years earlier reduced to providing color commentary for televised First Division matches.

Although it probably looks innocent and small-time by standards we Americans have cynically come to expect of our government officials, the English doomsayers were also treated to a whiff of graft and corruption among the bureaucracy, which was promptly explored in a series of Royal Commissions and judicial proceedings. One of the most rackety headlines involved a charge that a Labor member of Parliament had accepted a total of 250 pounds, or $645 U.S., about the price of nailing down an alderman's vote in a medium-size American city, for miscellaneous expenses over a period of ten years.

73

In the crisis condition thus created, those English gentlemen given to extravagant depressions even in the best of times stepped up the decibel count of their gloomy bombast. "The game is up, you know," a gent of impeccable credentials told me. "The Russians might just as well take over—if indeed they haven't taken over already. Chap at the club who hunted with the Duke a fortnight ago doesn't expect we can last another year."

The national malaise, in which we ourselves were almost swept up, was relieved only by further doses of about all England had to offer its suffering wards—more welfare and more pageantry. Old-age pensions increased; subsidies on bread and milk held the prices firm. At the same time, the diminishing shape of the future got papered over with more and more ceremonial ritual: Prince Charles's birthday, a Royal Tour abroad, race meets, wreath-layings, and Princess Anne's Royal Wedding, which caused such a stir that people thought of little else.

"She's a dear, isn't she?" a lady who works in the grocery in Bourton we frequently patronize said out of the blue one day. I knew very well who she meant, of course, but I refused to admit it.

"Yes, she is, thanks, and we've been married ten wonderful years now."

Every so often I get a spooky feeling that it won't be long before Old Blighty becomes a blithering comic opera state, all pomp and circumstance, without any influential ranking in the global community, endlessly diverting its people with more ceremonial parades, more changings of the guards, more Royal Tattoos by the ninety-seventh Hussars, Her Majesty's Upper Highlanders, Horse Blue Stalwarts; that sort of thing, God knows, is already all too frequent, while England's tattered prestige sinks to the level of, say, Italy. The prospect isn't especially frightening, I might add. On the basis of the American experience, superpowerdom isn't altogether beneficial.

Once the buzz over the Royal Wedding subsided, natives couldn't help but notice yet another curse rising to haunt them.

In sweet shops, chemists, and grocers they found essential goods in short supply or completely out of stock—corned beef, aftershave lotion, several kinds of canned food, milk, sugar, finally even toilet paper. While it lasted I bought several rolls of bootleg stuff in Bourton at the men's hairdresser, who never explained the source of a large supply he peddled off at something more than the normal going rate.

Although temporary shortages of those and other items struck me as a minor inconvenience in the full frame of events, it put many Englishmen we knew straight up the wall. Even with kitchen larders comfortably stocked, they saw a fearful vision of harder times to come. A national newspaper whose editorial judgment I generally respect waved the bloody flag with a purple essay running under a Is England Ready For a military Coup? headline.

Our own lives continued much the same despite the bewildering national problems. Having endured brownouts, blackouts, food shortages, rising prices, big-league corruption, strikes, blizzards, heat waves, and what the government back in America used to describe as rolling readjustments, not to mention the equivalent of the World Cup disaster when we lost the Olympic Games again, Joan and I took a detached view of things. If Armageddon amounted to nothing more than substituting Kleenex for proper toilet paper, we could carry on.

But the fell clutch of circumstance extended its arm again. With oil supplies still not running at the wanton old rate and diminishing coal reserves approaching critical levels as the strike action continued, Prime Minister Edward Heath finally took to television for one of those heart-to-hearts with the people. After a pointed reference to the Battle of Britain spirit that had sustained the country back in an even more ominous time, he got down to cases. In an effort to conserve electricity, which is generated largely from coal, of course, all commercial and public television would go dark at ten o'clock, the people would switch off heating units in rooms they weren't using, and British industry would be reduced immediately to a three-day work week.

The three-day week was a hammer blow for millions of English laborers. Three men in Slaughter who work factory jobs several miles away let it be known that they were available for handyman chores around the village, and one of them told me that he didn't know whether he could keep his family afloat on the half-time arrangement. A three-day week meant a three-day paycheck, and, needless to say, there were mortgages, hire purchase agreements, and other burdens to be met.

Oddly enough, although the austerity program was a blight for the bulk of the English, it had little or no effect on us or on many of the natives we knew. The fact that the telly went blank at ten wasn't the disaster it might seem, not with British programing little better than the standard American bill of fare. Milk, daily papers, and mail arrived at our cottage each morning, although the afternoon post was cancelled for the time being; I drove the car back and forth to my rented office on the same old five-day work schedule; we shopped and attended movies; and my weekly badminton in the school gymnasium in Bourton proceeded the same as always. Her Majesty's Government treated Scott to his regular allergy shots at no cost or obligation; several friends from home rode the train out from London tours for visits.

As a connoisseur of hard times—a Midwestern boyhood through the Great Depression, considerable time in Berlin, Frankfurt, Munich, and Vienna in the immediate postwar period, a busted year behind God's back in Africa—the British crunch was a breeze for me.

Although that latest turn of the screw seemed fairly remote despite some queasy guilt feelings that we weren't suffering as much as we probably ought to be on a share-and-share-alike basis, friends and relatives back home pictured the three of us teetering on the rim of doom. Nobody bothered sending any American newspapers along, but it was clear the papers and television weren't understating the situation. Otherwise the flutter of inbound letters and cards wouldn't have so consistently offered up excessive sympathy for all the hardships we surely were enduring.

One evening, after returning home from seeing the Newman-Redford film *The Sting*, I paid the baby-sitter her normal fee of a pound, or $2.50 U.S., and confected two lavish high cholesterol banana splits while Joan opened a sheaf of Christmas cards she hadn't gotten to earlier in the day. Shaking her head in wonder, occasionally laughing, she shuffled through kind but wildly inaccurate accompanying notes until she came upon one she couldn't resist reading aloud. After maybe five hundred despairing words on rising American prices, sagging American morale, and the fact that she devoted numerous hours shuttling from one service station to another in hopes of scrounging sufficient gasoline to make the wheels go round, a New Jersey friend acknowledged what she assumed to be our grim situation.

"But I'm not the one who should complain," she wrote. "You poor guys! We expect you'll be shipping back home very soon now."

As English Gentlemen and Players alike grumped on more than a three-day basis, the next step in the cliff-hanger became increasingly clear. All of a sudden the Heath government, like the soccer coach who became the ex-coach when the British side failed to qualify for the last split of the World Cup, made the sacrifice of calling a national election. During the fixed three-week campaign England's two major political parties exaggerated the philosophical fissures that divide them. But a funny thing happened on the way to 10 Downing Street. Officially neither party received a mandate. The Conservatives won more popular votes, and Labor won a few more seats in Parliament, and after hours of high-level confusion, Labor finally formed a fragile new government.

"All that campaign hoopla and you limeys didn't really vote anyone in," I kidded an English friend in Bourton.

"Better nobody than what you Yanks elected by a flaming big majority last time," he replied with devastating logic.

The new minority Harold Wilson Labor government quickly resolved several of England's most urgent problems. The coal strike was settled; the three-day week came to an end; sweeping economic and tax-reform measures went up to Parliament to a blast of Fleet Street trumpets. Although Labor's constituency generally went along with things—in the words of the late Yale football coach Herman Hickman, they were sullen, not mutinous —an incidental part of the original tax reform threatened to drive the thriving American community back to New Canaan, Bloomfield Hills, and Webster Groves unless it was whittled down. Instead of paying little or no English income taxes, foreign residents would be subject to normal British tax levels, which, with the National Health Service, nationalized railways, and other heavy industry and attendant costly welfare programs to finance, rank among the highest in the world.

In our own case, we hadn't chosen to settle in the United Kingdom because we saw it as a tax haven. It's perfectly true that Americans who live in England or any other foreign land for a period of at least eighteen months pay the U.S. Internal Revenue Service nothing on their first $20,000 of annual income, as happens with us. It's also perfectly true that Americans in England with a stake sufficient to live on, even in the form of a big-wink bank loan while salary checks are deposited in the same stateside bank, are beyond the reach of Inland Revenue and hence pay no English taxes, either.

We weren't playing that particular game, but we did feel the shock waves of the tax pronouncement. Some figuring in the new math indicated that we might have to pay around 40 percent of our total income in British taxes, which would be so prohibitive as to force us to leave, much as we were enjoying life as Yanks near Oxford.

In those worrisome days I received a letter from a New Yorker I used to work for who has an eye for the fine print. Toward the end of an amiable, chatty note he casually said the old Royal upright typewriter I formerly played still awaited me if the need arose. I replied in a tentative sort of way.

But under pressure from various groups, not the least of them the powerful U.S. Chamber of Commerce chapter in London, the new government soon scaled its tax reform as it related to foreigners down to reasonable size. Foreign residents would be taxed at the British rate all right, but on only 50 percent of their annual income, wherever it rolled up, which meant we would actually contribute less than the total outlay we previously sent off to IRS, New York State, and New York City.

In addition to the heartening tax-reform reform for outlanders, England's chronic crisis seemed to improve somewhat. Several essentials remained in short supply; the balance of payments deficit read like the Judgment Book; prices continued to accelerate, although nothing like the astonishing 3.7 percent figure the U.S. consumer price index rose in September. Nonetheless, the situation was noticeably brighter, as even English Gentlemen were compelled to admit when they clipped their Havanas and conjured up the familiar old hobgoblins.

By the end of our first full year in residence we noticed that an occasional Player had developed the habit of grumping, just like their social superiors. Every so often these freshly minted social critics, their skins gone woefully thin through long months of jangling crises, snap at well-meaning strangers who don't show the proper degree of respect for ornamental institutions they desperately cling to for lack of more meaningful handholds. For example, while the crisis was blowing at full level, an American visitor and I in a pub over in next-door Stow fell to discussing a newspaper picture of Queen Elizabeth. Despite my perpetual availability for lawn parties at Buckingham Palace, I've no way of knowing whether the likeness was accurate or not, but pictorially it was a disaster.

"She looks plain dowdy, with teeth some royal dentist ought to fold back a good bit," I told my guest.

"How's that, matey?"

A red-faced young citizen who appeared big and strong enough to be a British international rugby star provided he could remember the signals rose up from an adjoining table where he'd been topping up with the local beer as he eavesdropped.

"Well, I say this particular picture wouldn't win a beauty contest, would it?" I replied, throttling down some without really altering the basic message.

"You're insulting The Queen, matey. I don't like anyone insults The Queen. All you Canadians think you can bucket over here and insult The Queen and I . . . ."

As that authority on good manners moved menacingly toward us, his huge boots clumping on the floor, the proprietor of the pub and a confederate tugged at him, and, since I was almost done with my beer, I saw no reason to prolong the discussion. Out we went, fairly quickly too, in case the bristling pile of meat embarked on a quid pro quo tactic by denouncing Canadian Prime Minister Pierre Trudeau, whose appearance and honor, while undoubtedly true blue, I wasn't quite up to defending.

Chapter 8

"Pricey, very pricey." A neighbor named Walter Clifford lurched into his customary peroration as we fished a private lake stuffed with trout one soft twilight not long after our sabbatical began. "Things have gotten very pricey, haven't they?"

If Clifford, a vigorous, affable country squire blessed with far more of the world's goods than most others, isn't exactly typical of Lower Slaughter's 191 residents, his reaction emphatically was. In their narrow, honey-colored stone cottages snug under steep slate rooftops friends and neighbors grumble about little else.

It's perfectly true that prices have inflated throughout the United Kingdom in recent years. The economic blight has jacked up the price of essentials as assorted as kidney pie, electricity, and warm draft beer. In seven high-rolling years the diminutive cottage the Halifax Building Society helped us buy tripled in value quite apart from various creature comforts we added, including central heating.

Even the occasional local poachers ask a bit more for the rustled trout they flog out behind cafés in nearby villages. Over in Shipston-on-Stour, eleven miles away, Billy Hudson, the town crier, has raised his prices too. He now offers up a deafening commercial word on behalf of local fetes, auctions, and sales for no less than 50 pence, or $1.25 U.S., for the usual twenty cries in the early evening.

For an itinerant American long accustomed to the price levels back in New York City, however, not to mention the hellish bite in a rural community in upstate New York where we used to restore our id every summer, family balance sheets are a breeze. Midway through our stay a loaf of homemade bread came to 20¢ U.S.; we had a choice of four first-run movies in Cheltenham for $1 U.S. admission; and the woodmonger personally delivered twenty fireplace logs for 50¢ U.S. Given a native economy pegged to prices like these, my wife, whose manifold virtues specifically don't include an austerity gland, isn't going to win any Homemaker-of-the-Year awards merely because she makes do with a weekly food allotment of sixteen pounds, 50 pence, or $41.25 U.S.

Every once in a while I admit to getting caught up in all the shock and alarm regarding the rising pattern of prices. On a relative scale it never amounted to that much. The increase was so modest compared to what we'd been suffering in New York that it was no real concern.

As a dramatic case in point, I embarked on a market survey two days before we fled Manhattan to establish some standards we could apply. At the supermarket that we regularly patronized I filled the cart with twenty-one basic items: milk, margarine, lettuce, eggs, boiled ham, that sort of thing. Total cost: $14.46, including sales tax.

Exactly a week later I set off in Bourton-on-the-Water in search of similar provisions. The cost of the same twenty-one items—cornflakes by Kellogg, instant coffee by Nescafé—ran the equivalent of $8.68, no tax, although England's new 8 percent value-added tax applies to virtually everything other than foodstuffs. That afternoon I asked a cobbler if he could stitch up a worn toe-sprung old pair of L. L. Bean slippers. He could. For the sake of my curiosity I timed him once he turned on the machinery: fourteen minutes flat.

"How much?" Joan said on my return.

"You wouldn't believe it."

"Well, how much?"

"Ten pence."

"What's that in our money?"

"Twenty-five cents. A quarter. Two bits."

"Don't tell Jack Stewart." She mentioned a very snug friend. "He'll start packing."

If the gap seemed excessive at the time we first settled in England, it became more excessive still as the summer wore on. At the end of our first month official figures released in Washington, D.C., suggested that we'd abandoned ship just in time. In that thirty-day period the cost of provisions in America had grown by a whopping 6.1 percent, the largest monthly increase since 1917, no matter what gramps says about the good old days.

The fact that groceries are so inexpensive by American standards hasn't escaped the notice of prudent U.S. Air Force families assigned to the base at neighboring Upper Heyford. In time they discover that the going rates at the PX and commissary aren't necessarily so rock-bottom as they thought, although they do the bulk of their shopping in those discount marts because frozen waffles, Sara Lee cakes, Mounds bars, and other familiar down-home provisions aren't generally available in England.

By selective shopping, however, Air Force families manage to get the best of both worlds: root beer and black cherry Jell-o at the commissary, fresh vegetables, homemade bread, eggs, lettuce, and some cuts of fresh meats at civilian shops in the small adjoining villages they inhabit. "English butter, and I mean real English butter, nothing better, either, sells for the equivalent of fifty-some cents a pound in our village shop," Joe Rickey, a sergeant whose formidable girth visibly qualifies him as an authority, told me. "At the commissary we pay just over eighty cents for stockpile butter from home."

Selective shopping has been known to pay the occasional dividend for us, too. Normally fresh potatoes are 2, 2½, or 3 pence, or between 5¢ and 7½¢ U.S., a pound. Now we buy in volume, what the English call half a hundredweight for 60 pence, which means starch runs us about 3¢ U.S. the pound. At the risk of throwing my spinal column out of whack we also patronize pick-them-yourself berry fields in season, 10 pence, or 25¢ U.S., a quart for raspberries or strawberries.

Anyone who suspects that the cost of food in English shops isn't typical of the cost in cafés and restaurants shouldn't. Except for London, where price studies have no real meaning anyway, the same comfortable difference between England and the United States is apparent any time a couple decides to abandon the family cooker, or stove, for a round of boiled dinner somewhere. At any one of three cafés near the office I rent, three-course luncheons are available for around $2, or far less than I was paying in New York. Unless I wanted to jeopardize the diminishing state of my health at a stand-up Manhattan trap whose name, "Munchtime USA," is as offensive as its bill of fare, I seldom was able to manage even an elemental feeding for less than $4.

In England the price gap isn't restricted to groceries. Annual rates, or taxes, on our two-bedroom cottage are fixed at thirty-two pounds, or $89 U.S.; an eighty-two-mile bus ride to London runs 80 pence, or $2 U.S.; a chiropractor bills me (chiropractors are private vendors, not part of the government National Health Service) 50 pence, or $1.25 U.S., for the same periodic agonies with a rebellious toenail that cost $10 in New York City. Along with everything else, a standard Milky Way candy bar still retails for 2 pence, or 5¢ U.S., a nickel, in case anyone still remembers that coin.

Despite the generally modest price levels overall by our standards, hardcover books, electricity, postage, liquor, cigarettes, and several other expenditures come to approximately the same as they do in America. Prices for just about anything in London are chilling, almost as much as Chicago or New York, which explains why we don't weekend in the antique old capital city as much as we'd like.

If the cost of gasoline is about double the going rate in America, with everyone suffering except the major oil companies whose earnings go up, up, up, the actual cost of driving runs about the same in England and the United States. An anomaly? Not really. What balances things out is the fact that four-cylinder English cars get thirty to thirty-five miles to the gallon, whereas our eight-cylinder convertible at home never did as much as fifteen even on a turnpike at something close to legal speeds. Happily, comprehensive insurance, oil changes, and repairs are less.

After gazing at sleek new Jaguars and Daimlers, Rovers and Triumphs, we scaled our dream down to proper size and bought a basic four-door Vauxhall with three years and 40,000 miles on it. The car doesn't measure up as a status symbol, but at least the $1,200 investment proved to be perfectly adequate transport. It burns little oil, runs around thirty-two miles per gallon, and seldom misbehaves.

Even a complication I feared might cost me the price of a new tennis racket was surprisingly little. When the battery went flat one wintry morning I rang up the garage for help. Out they came, two mechanics riding a repair van, carrying a toolbox and a spare battery. They got the car started, prudently followed me to the garage, and set to work. The total bill for the rescue mission, a battery charge, a tune-up, new plugs, and two gallons of antifreeze was three pounds, 50 pence, or $8.70 U.S.

Another time I stove in the left rear door watching a dream of a girl instead of the small bridge I was driving across. On the basis of several melancholy past experiences it looked like $200 in New York City and $150 in upstate Grahamsville.

"Take it straight to the panel-basher in Bourton," an eyewitness advised me.

On arriving at what can only be described as a flourishing place of business, narrow British roadways being what they are, I was dismayed to see the panel-basher circle the car, carefully examine the ruined door, and sadly shake his head, like the doctors in old Hollywood movies when they were quizzed about the patient's condition.

"Take me half a day to hammer this one out, and then refit the door, and paint the whole thing over, one coat, probably two, plus stripping, won't it?" He scratched on a pad. "Say the job will run around twelve pounds."

It did too. Twelve pounds translates into $30 U.S. The bill struck me as astonishing, yet several friends failed to see it that way. Typically, my neighbor Walter Clifford put a different interpretation on the experience when I asked whether he didn't agree that it was surprisingly fair.

"Pricey, very pricey," he said, right on cue.

Americans who go bust riding cabs might be interested in the going rate out our way. After a savage hour in the dental chair one afternoon Joan decided that she wasn't up to toddling all the way back to the cottage. The fare to our doorstep, which I later clocked at exactly 2.1 miles, came to 30 pence, or 75¢ U.S., no tip. Why spoil the natives?

But a chronic inflation continued during most of our stay. It kept bulging through two different governments, and though the rate wasn't much worse than that in America, it was a problem all the same. Every so often the grim specter of having to cut back critical annual budget categories like entertainment ($1,000), new clothes ($1,000) or the board chairman's fishing ($300)—we overran our total annual budget of $11,600 by only $712 the first year —rose up to haunt us.

Even an incident so trivial as an increase in citrus shook me more than it should have. For weeks I had been buying lovely oranges shipped all the way from South Africa at 2 pence, or

5¢ U.S., each, which struck me as such a bargain that I kept a supply in the trunk of the car in case I felt like quartering one after a brisk, if pattycake, round of tennis. After all, oranges shipped from Florida to New York City used to sell for 15, 20, and even 25¢ each, which made them almost as precious as they must have been at the turn of the century in Illinois when my mother used to receive one fresh orange and maybe a new pair of mittens for Christmas.

The first time I noticed a new sign on the orange bin at the green grocery the 3 pence price tag bothered me some without seeming prohibitive. At the time I still mentally calibrated prices in American currency. A penny amounted to a penny—no more. But on reflecting some I came to realize that while a price jump from two to three pence didn't look like much, it actually meant an increase from 5¢ to 7½¢ in the American currency I'd spent most of my career accumulating so very little of.

At 7½¢, the cost of a fresh orange from South Africa was still substantially less than a fresh orange from Florida, but it no longer seemed a great bargain, and we stopped casually buying them in large quantities. As for the cache I previously kept in the boot of the car for restorative purposes following tennis, I discovered that a load of malt at a spot called the Coach and Horses had it all over citrus anyway.

During all that time inflation in America also kept driving upward at an accelerating rate, despite a series of what the president whimsically called game plans. Letters from home—soon the price of postage went up too, I noticed—became so lachrymose that I probably should have tied on a rubber bib before opening the morning mail.

Eventually Joan and I hit on the loony notion of a transatlantic price competition. Any time a correspondent friend let out an anguished whoop about the cost of something or other in the United States, we then bought the same item in a local shop and made a point of including the English price in our reply.

One day my brother in Los Angeles reported that fresh lettuce was going at 85¢ a pop. At a green grocery we picked up a splendid head for 6 pence, or 15¢ U.S.

A fishing chum from New York mentioned the cost of flies in a letter otherwise devoted to an epic trout he'd have driven straight to the taxidermist if only the 4x leader hadn't snapped off: 85¢ each. At a neighboring tackle shop I picked up a dozen lovely silver butcher flies at 10 pence, or 25¢ U.S., each.

A friend in New York, a financial writer for the *New York Times*, in fact, whose interest in the subject was thus professional as well as purely personal, interrupted the flow of a gossipy note to complain that premium bacon was up to $1.80 a pound. At a specialty food shop two miles away an affable menial sliced us a pound of bacon, number four cut, for 36 pence, or 90¢ U.S.

And so it went. A friend in Detroit reported paying $2.89 a pound for fresh loin lamb chops, which our butcher sells for $1.75; a boyhood acquaintance as much of a tosspot as I am in the matter of milk moaned the 47¢ a quart, while we paid the equivalent of 22¢ U.S. per quart for what we find in old-fashioned glass bottles on our doorstep six mornings a week; a writer in Boston grumped about 48¢ package bread, while we pay 9 pence, or 22¢ U.S., for a loaf of homemade.

Far and away the most effective instance occurred when a couple from Aurora, Illinois, arrived in the English countryside for a visit. In ticking off a list of vile prices in Illinois, the husband happened to mention that resident barbers there received $3 plus whatever they could wheedle in the form of a tip for a standard trim. Although my friend wasn't especially in need of a haircut, with the hand of God eroding his hairline for him, I drove him straight to my regular barber in Stow-on-the-Wold, who gave him a full cut, along with the blithering monologue so endemic among barbers everywhere, for 30 pence, or 75¢ U.S. Although I cautioned him against it, my extravagant guest was so warmed by what seemed a benefit performance by the $3 standards he was accustomed to that he tipped him 10 pence, or 25¢ U.S., which didn't establish the Yanks-in-England precedent the barber probably hoped it would next time I dropped by.

Actually the whole range of tips and gratuities is so modest I almost hesitate to go into detail for fear I might lose credibility. Our last Christmas season in Manhattan we distributed $119 to an assortment of apartment house doormen, postmen, the superintendent, the milkman, the part-time cleaning lady, and staff help at two clubs I belong to. Our first Yule in Lower Slaughter cash grants for the milkman, the dustmen, the chimney sweep, the postmen, and the cleaning lady came to a total—a total, mind you—of three pounds, 50 pence, or $8.75 U.S., which is enough to make a grown man start believing in Father Christmas, as the English call Santa Claus.

Prices up and down the line are spectacular enough for us to indulge passions we simply couldn't afford in America. We pay 75 pence, or $1.87 U.S., for riding lessons for our son, including the use of the horse; seven pounds, or $17.50 U.S., is the monthly rental for a commodious office whose double windows overlook a rose garden, an orchard, and, out beyond, seven cows grazing a green pasture; and seventy-five pounds, or $187.50 U.S., is the yearly cost for my share of over a mile of marvelous salmon water on the River Wye in Wales. At the risk of offending my man Sid at Chipp's on East Forty-fourth Street in Manhattan, it's only fair to report that I invested less than $40 U.S. for an odd jacket in four-star Donegal tweed.

If anything, the upkeep on my defective backhand amounts to an even greater saving. On the basis of a prudent word here, a judicious word there, I let it be known that I'd agree to join the Bourton Vale Tennis Club—two nice hard courts, a small clubhouse, even a cooker for brewing tea—just two miles away, or about the same distance I used to travel to make a fool of myself every Tuesday night in New York City.

Weeks later, a lady who identified herself as the club secretary phoned with the news that I'd been accepted for membership. After she courteously told me where the keys to the outer gate were kept, the schedule of club matches, and a stiff club rule about wearing only whites, I thought it was time to raise The Big Question. Gently as I could, I asked what initiation and dues might run.

"Oh yes," she said. "Three pounds, ten."

Numbly I tried to relate $7.75 U.S. to price levels I'd known before, $10 an hour court rental in Illinois, $26 an hour in mid-Manhattan, plus incidental fiddles like $35 annual locker fees.

"Fine," I said. "Is that for a week or a month?"

"No, no." The club secretary softly cleared her throat. "The three pounds, ten is the subscription for the full season."

"Oh."

"Of course there is one other thing," she continued. Here it comes, I figured, a forehand drive with lots of topspin to it, a three-figure contribution to the building fund, something like that. "Any time you bring a nonmember guest you pay an additional fee of 2 pence."

The price of a night on the town is wonderfully reasonable, too. Back in New York City we scheduled all too few evenings out due to prohibitive costs. With an initial investment of $8 to $10 for a baby-sitter, even hamburgers selling at roughly the price of Standard Oil, and movies running $4 a ticket, a modest happening came to around $25, which was why we normally wore out the upholstery on our living room sofa reading, tracking television, or entertaining friends.

Consider a potluck ride into the night here in rural England. Our baby-sitter charges a flat rate of one pound, or $2.50 U.S., no matter how late we check in; tickets to first-run movies cost 40 pence, or $1 U.S.; chicken-in-the-basket and fish-and-chips cuisine run about the same. Unless we stake everyone in sight to a round of drinks at Lords of the Manor afterward, the whole thing seldom exceeds $10.

While entertainment, recreation, food, wearing apparel and most other basics are inexpensive by stateside standards, the biggest bargain of all involves the people, reliable, hard-working people, who provide the services we previously couldn't afford. In New York a bright, downbeat world class cleaning lady, worth her weight in silver polish, came by every Monday for $24 plus bus fare.

Here in Slaughter we have equally stalwart domestic help in the form of a lady who stops by three hours every morning, five mornings a week, cleaning, sweeping, dusting, mopping, vacuuming, washing up, scrubbing floors, making beds, polishing brass and silver, even contributing some old-fashioned ironing when the need arises. We pay her just five pounds, or $12.50 U.S., a week, although a neighbor with long experience in these matters chidingly told us that was a bit much.

Actually the coolie wage scale would have startled us even more if it hadn't been for a revealing preview of things to come soon after we settled in England. Once I managed to find office space I booked a haulier chap to come round and wrestle twenty-three boxes and crates filled mostly with books, weighing around fifty pounds each, to the office. The cheerful broad-beamed man drew up his car and van to the house, loaded the crates, drove the two miles, unloaded the burden, and neatly stacked the crates along one wall of the office, all for one pound, $2.50 U.S., or about the price of a cab from East Seventy-first Street to the bank in the Grand Central area that covers my overdrafts.

With a little luck it's possible to dial in both goods and services at those discount rates, as I've done several times, especially the day I realized that I needed some secondhand bookshelves for the office. I took my problem to Billy, a bouncy bespectacled handyman no bigger than a ferret, an ex-Londoner, who listened carefully and said, "Right, guv. I'll have a go." Two days later he knocked on my window with a progress report. He'd found a shelf five feet high and six feet long for two pounds, or $5 U.S.

Next morning, Billy was awaiting me, the enormous bookshelf roped up on his bicycle, which he had pushed a distance of five miles. When I asked what I owed, he said it was up to me. In retrospect my offering of four pounds, or $10 U.S., seems frugal for all his time and effort, including his two pound cash outlay. But Billy didn't see it that way.

"Too much, guv." He returned a pound note. "I don't want to make a fortune off you, do I?"

Like other Americans happily doing time in the United Kingdom the state of our solvency depends to some extent on the dollar-sterling exchange rate, which can fluctuate widely. First thing every morning—well, second thing, anyway—I check the rate in the morning paper before my vision goes hazy trying to track U.S. baseball scores in agate type hidden away somewhere in the sports section.

At the time we arrived in England in July of 1973, a combination of events—Watergate, a wounded stock market, soaring interest rates, inflation, a whopping deficit in the trade balance, a jittery feeling generally—had withered the greenback to some historic lows. Despite a downward revaluation some months before and rumors that it might be devalued again, that wonderful old absolute, the dollar, was catching hell in the international marketplace.

Fortunately for us, if not for a host of vacationers bound for other parts of the world, notably France, West Germany, and Switzerland, American currency suffered less in England than it did elsewhere. British sterling was almost as soft. Still, official rates fixed the pound sterling at $2.58 the day we arrived, or around 7 percent off the $2.40 we originally hoped for and on which the hairline budget we'd concocted that spring was pinned.

The limited capital we carried along was in the form of several Chase Manhattan Bank drafts, each of them for $5,000, which I planned to deposit in our checking account in an English bank, in full view of England's Inland Revenue vigilantes, to prove, if necessary, that we had the funds to sustain ourselves without me doing too much serious commercial writing. Since our resident bank balance was practically nil, I converted one of the $5,000 drafts into sterling at the exorbitant $2.58 rate.

After a crash meeting with my wife there in the bank lobby I decided to speculate some by not converting more of our dollar capital into sterling. Sooner or later, I told myself, the dollar would recover—and then I'd rush into London waving another $5,000 bank draft and convert it at a price rather better than the distressing low recorded the day of our arrival.

As things turned out, that was precisely what happened. Several weeks later I cashed a second at $2.46 the pound, and late in the fall I cashed another at $2.42. Although the fluctuations might not appear to be that excessive, the $2.42 figure stretched the $5,000 almost $350 over what the $2.58 fetched.

As things also turned out, however, I should have held out a while longer. Through the winter England's headline economic crunch, featuring the coal miners' strike and the three-day work week, seriously defrosted the pound, which naturally gave the dollar far more bounce, as television newscasts informed people, including my wife.

"The dollar is a lot better, isn't it?" she said one evening.

"Some." If I sounded defensive, I had every reason to.

"How much better?"

"A good bit, actually."

"Exactly how much?" Her voice was strung with icicles.

"Well, the pound is a record two dollars, eighteen-and-a-half cents today."

"And no more patriotic old Yankee greenbacks to convert?"

"Not too many."

Yet toward the end of our first year in England bewildering economic forces I don't pretend to comprehend set the dollar to reeling and sterling to improving, or both. As the beneficiary of some windfall money, I wanted to convert it to wipe out our remaining mortgage payments and to buy a mint condition Austin Princess sedan fitted with a Rolls-Royce engine, but the exchange rate ominously ticked up: $2.39, $2.40, $2.41, $2.42.

Under these circumstances, wincing and almost crying aloud,

I was obviously entitled to what in our warped perspective could be interpreted as some good news. In it came, bingo, a stricken letter from my brother in California, who happens to be so thrifty, if not downright parsimonious, that he's been said to throw dimes around like manhole covers. In describing a shopping splurge by his standards, Jack wrote that he had bought a half gallon of milk, six cans of cola, and a small packet of Kraft cheese.

"Would you believe $5.02?" he wrote. "Better stay right where you are, limey."

Spot on. Limey it is.

Chapter 9

Any adult with an IQ equal to his body temperature installs a
television set soon after taking up residence in England if only
to warm the lounge, as they call the living room over here,
through the long raw winter. As a practicing adult with an IQ
at least the equal of my body temperature, although both figures
tend to fluctuate some lately, I made the customary arrangements
once we settled in.

In England customary arrangements can be a bit flexible. In
our case we priced the new twenty-inch sets at a neighboring
electricmonger, 80 pounds, or $200 U.S., and up for black-and-
white; 230 pounds, or $575 U.S., for living color. As vagabonds
over on only a two-year pass, we prudently decided to rent a basic
black-and-white for two pounds, 17 pence, or $5.22 U.S., per
month instead, which also whittled down the risk factor. Any
subsequent aches and pains—such as a new picture tube transplant—would be on the house.

In Old Blighty the rental or purchase price of a telly, plus the cost of the juice to light it up, doesn't cover the total investment, as several neighbors quickly cautioned us when a stalwart chap in bib overalls finally got around to rolling our set through the front door. Her Majesty's Government, to whom so many such assorted blessings flow, puts the arm on every devotee in the form of an annual license fee. An automatic fine of 50 pounds, or $125 U.S., is sufficient to discourage any prospective wrongdoers, including this one.

Even so, I did feel compelled to file what I still consider an appropriate objection on stopping by the post office to pay my dues.

"Since I'm obliged to pay this tax I never had the opportunity to vote on, I might arrange to dump all the tea into Boston Harbor," I said in a light-hearted voice.

"What's that you're saying about tea, please," the woman behind the window inquired blankly, as several people queued up behind me ground what remained of their teeth. Outnumbered by redcoats who didn't quite grasp my reference, I paid the seven pounds, or $17.50 U.S., whereupon it seemed legal to jigger the dials.

Back in New York City, Channel 13, our local public broadcasting station, had treated us to fine BBC import drama, droll comedy, and stimulating public affairs discussions. On the basis of that heady brew we expected our rental screen to glow with magic.

Unfortunately the magic has been in very short supply. Despite a number of glaring differences between England and the United States, a despairing similarity exists. Both countries serve up a sodden television bill of fare that captive viewers gulp down rather than demand a better substitute.

Except for the occasional drama of high distinction or the infrequent brilliant documentary that must have slipped through by accident, both BBC and the commercial channels offer a humdrum potpourri of wind-up domestic comedies, noisy game shows, crime adventures, and old, old movies, most of them Hollywood confections.

During our first summer, British television seemed to be saluting that classic mummer and upright American, John Wayne. The screen filled up with John Wayne, as combat pilot, cowboy, construction company troubleshooter, soldier of fortune. Although the Wayne films were potboilers—what else?—they might be described as artistic triumphs compared to the average run of movies shipped to England from the United States. Ever watch Ray Milland, of all people, in a low-budget Western? We did, only not for long. The titles themselves—*Tanganyika, Untamed, Band of Angels, The St. Valentine's Day Massacre, Denver and Rio Grande, Tarzan and the Trappers*—illustrate the sort of American film that British television moguls ought to ship straight back marked "Opened By Mistake."

Along with those and other full-length disasters, British television is awash with dated stateside programs so inane that I'd be concerned about the state of Anglo-American understanding if the native rubbish didn't happen to be equally bad. Apart from the flat sameness of the story line, Raymond Burr's "Ironside" series is fairly good stuff, but some evenings more than half the prime time is given over to such taffy as "Petticoat Junction," "Streets of San Francisco," "I Dream of Jeannie," "The Partridge Family," "Hawaii Five-O," and the assembly-line adventures of the FBI. Those diversions don't travel any better than one would expect.

As if the substandard run of imported American celluloid isn't bad enough, my wife and I almost took the pledge the night when, while we casually spun the dial, the image of something called "Bridget Loves Bernie" flickered on the screen. In New York City that was the sort of thing that used to make us wonder about trading our set in for a color radio.

Although Love It or Leave It Americans often fault the British for their elegant ways, their superior airs, their stiff upper rectitude, we have found few of those qualities in their own situation comedies. I'm hard put to single out the most offensive entry, but it might be "Casanova," a crude, leering series about a philandering husband trying to seduce some toothsome wench while his hip wife ingeniously seeks to thwart his plans.

But one point must be made for British television. No matter how aimless, idiotic, or vulgar the script, the performances are superb. From the lead right on down to the hotel doormen, the acting strikes me as having far more style and wit than our casual American performing, impressive as it sometimes can be.

By now millions of Americans blessed with public broadcasting stations are familiar with the best of English drama. It is beautifully written, intelligently directed, and magnificently acted; and many of the stories have searing and powerful themes. If the script requires that two people be filmed in bed, all right, very well, there they are. The cameras don't focus on the dimmed lamp or a thunderstorm rattling the bedroom windows, with the background orchestra segueing into Ravel's *Bolero*. Whatever its faults, television is honest and mature in England.

Yet our indentured screen also fills with a sodden stew of game and quiz shows: "Sale of the Century," "Full House," "House Party," "It's a Knockout," "The Generation Game," "Whose Baby," "Opportunity Knocks." Regional variations for Welsh audiences include "Heddiw," "y Dydd," "Miri Mawr."

One thing the British do fairly well is the documentary, including a number of on-the-scene reports from America, on which the cameras have frequently fixed a merciless eye. "The Lord Is My Shepherd and He Knows I'm Gay" opened with a cheap trick scene of two homosexuals saying their vows in an elaborate church wedding, complete with nuptial kiss. But thereafter the film settled down to an absorbing and understanding account of California's gay population, which included a bewildered transsexual father on the verge of becoming a grandmother. The closing shots of a moving memorial service mourning the death of fellow homosexuals killed in a fire deliberately set by hardhat moralists were hard to bear watching.

Any time the supply of documentaries, drama, situation comedies, game shows, and Hollywood films runs low, news shows appear. Except for the accents, newscasts are much like the daily headline summaries witnessed by viewers back home, but with commentators reading cardboard bulletins at their desks, sports scores cast in English—"Leeds one, Manchester City nil"—and trite on-the-spot interviews with actual newsmakers.

Soon after we settled in Lower Slaughter a suspenseful human drama involving two Englishmen trapped on the floor of the North Atlantic in a defective midget submarine was unfolding, and at the peak of it a straight news interview came over as wildly comic. Even today the handwritten notes I filed at the time the BBC commentator got hold of an executive of Vickers Oceanic Ltd. read like a Bob and Ray sketch.

Reporter: "Would you say that this is the most crucial phase of the rescue operation?"

Man from Vickers: "Yes, I'd say this is the most crucial phase of the *entire* rescue operation."

Reporter: "Would the chances be fairly good that the rescue will succeed?"

Man from Vickers: "I can assure you that the chances are *quite* good that the rescue will succeed."

Although a literal and straightforward approach to the news isn't to my taste, the same no-nonsense approach to the weather most emphatically is. Mercifully, the British do without the long preliminary windup that used to bother me back home—thunderheads building up in northern Montana, cold fronts in Tuscaloosa, scattered squalls in the Great Lakes, complete with maps, arrows, circles, and a pointer. The English get right to the point with a brief forecast of tomorrow's weather accompanied by the probable temperature in both Centigrade and Fahrenheit, but don't bet on it. For obvious reasons, the stress is a bit different: "Some sunny spells."

Unless the news from the States is positively thunderous, it isn't a regular part of the evening news. Many times we watch a full half-hour of the stuff without so much as a mention of anything from Washington, which, the way things have been going there, is probably just as well.

If the resident medium offers any distinguished fare besides the occasional marvelous drama or documentary, it comes in the realm of sports coverage, which consumes approximately as many hours as fun and games do there in the colonies. Any time a major horse show, international cricket match, or big-money golf tournament takes place, producers let the coverage run on and on. Significant moments are enshrined with what they call action replays. On weekend afternoons the miscellaneous fishing, cycling, logrolling, and such served up by "Grandstand" and "World of Sports" even included Howard Cosell calling a Mohammed Ali prizefight, which made me a bit wistful despite the usual nasal platitudes.

But sometimes the hyperbolic build-up before the big game becomes downright silly. One springtime we were treated not only to interviews with players, wives and children, coaches, trainers, groundskeepers, ex-players, journalists, and others before England's professional soccer championship but also to a loony visit with a licensed astrologist, whose star-kissed choice promptly lost the match three to nil.

Although my wife never managed to grasp the situation in its full horror, I can't forget a high spot of the televised coverage of the Royal Horse Show our first full summer in Old Blighty. I don't pretend any expertise in the matter of horse shows, understand, but my youthful years playing a variety of games did qualify me as an authority for what I saw on the screen.

In one event riders went over the jumps bareback, without even thin saddles, their knees pressed tight against the flanks of their horses as they went up, up, up over the barriers. Inevitably, I suppose, one unfortunate rider came down too hard against his horse. He rolled off, writhed in the sawdust, and then crawled over to a rail where he bent double in the ancient pose, his face a mask of suffering.

Despite visible evidence to the contrary, an urbane announcer doing the commentary felt called upon to offend no sensibilities among the viewers.

"It looks as if Boyd banged himself on the knee, doesn't it?" he improvised, a mendacity that brought a whoop of laughter from my seat in our lounge.

"What's so funny?" Joan inquired.

"Banged himself in the jewels is what happened," I said.

To his credit, the commentator, not to mention a colleague assigned to supply the color, couldn't help but burst into occasional laughter himself as he described subsequent events in the competition.

As the father of a son entitled to a daily ration of television if he wants, as he generally does, it probably isn't surprising that I've kept him company during some of the entertainment. Since he sees "Scooby-Doo," "The Flintstones," "Yogi Bear," "Josie and the Pussycats," and all too many other imported programs he also watched in America, culture shock was held to a minimum.

But the British are capable of turning out some impressive children's programs of their own. "Black Beauty," "Vision On," "Blue Peter," "Jackonary," and "Magic Roundabout" are entertaining shows, while an afternoon newscast specifically beamed at youngsters struck me as so clever I leaned on a network friend in New York to plagiarize or acquire domestic rights to the idea. There is a gentle, thoughtful quality in much of the children's fare that we, as parents, find reassuring.

For all the many similarities between English and U.S. television, emphatic differences regarding the choice of channels exist. In Lower Slaughter we have a choice of exactly two channels, BBC1 and ATV, instead of the eight or nine we dialed in New York City, although neighbors with stronger, more expensive aerials on their slate rooftops can also bring in BBC2.

Reception on our set is reasonably good, except that sometimes BBC1 temporarily goes white as a stray car drums along the narrow roadway outside the cottage. But BBC1 more than makes up for that by running all its shows without a single commercial word intruding, a wonderful treat, especially with English commercial words on the other commercial channel being even less fun and more toxic than what we used to complain about on East Seventy-first Street.

We can't help but consider the lack of an endless barrage of brief messages from the sponsor a major victory, of course, but the informal, erratic timetable drives me up the nearest dry stone wall. The daily television listings read like a railway schedule: 7:12, 8:25, 9:20. After years of conditioning myself to see the ten o'clock news at exactly that time, it's difficult catching the daily log of disaster at 9:53 one night and maybe 10:08 the next.

The fact that English television is little, if any, better than the cause of our eyestrain back home is perplexing with English radio so wonderfully good. Joan and I leaned on BBC's Radio One through Four to a point where one of the most fractious domestic scenes we've endured came about the night we got to blaming each other for forgetting to lay in a supply of fresh batteries for a transistor radio that had suddenly gone dead.

The dramas, panel discussions, whodunits, poetry, comedies, good music, and even long-running soaps like "The Archers," constantly remind me that radio can still amount to an addictive art form of the sort that caused me to breach strict house rules by smuggling a crystal set into bed back in my lost youth. More recently, alas, the American brand of radio in whose wave lengths we lived consisted of a beggar's choice between monotonous round-the-clock news headlines in no depth and generation gap-type electric guitars forever playing the same nonsong.

At this longitude radio treats us to something more than BBC if we choose. At night, while telly screens bristle with diversions like "Moonbase," "Doctors in Charge," and "Coronation Street," our small Sony pulls in programs in several languages, among them American, such as Voice of America newscasts pegged to events at home and Armed Forces Network pegged mostly to rock music and sports. But if Armed Forces wants to sustain the morale of the lads manning freedom's outposts abroad by injecting them with a daily ration of play-by-play, I'm perfectly willing to join in—in, mind you, not up—only I wish the running commentaries wouldn't invariably fade away just when my blood pressure starts to drum. In one agonizing case the suspense continued for two full days before the Paris *Herald Tribune* finally ran the score of a showdown Giant-Dodger thriller that the radio had tuned out during the top of the ninth, 2–2 tie score, Dodgers at bat, two on, and two out.

As anyone with a working eardrum knows, England's state radio network doesn't shirk its civic commitment to the elementals, else Radio One wouldn't run programs entitled "Top Ten Hits," "Bryan Ferry's Top 12," "Tom Browne with the Top 20," and, dear God, even "Your 100 Best Tunes." But radio is often up to far better things. On a good day the options include discussion shows on inflation, angling, and paleontology; dramatic adaptations of *The Cherry Orchard, Quo Vadis,* and *The Pass Beyond Kashmir;* reports from Parliament, the stock market, and America; and series on Lord Byron, the poet, Lord Douglas-Home, the former foreign secretary, and Lord Dracula.

Every weeknight BBC radio also stands listeners to a popular long-running feature called "Book at Bedtime," with someone from the Radio Registry who doesn't suffer from glottal stops doing a fifteen-minute turn reading aloud from a novel by Edna Ferber, Somerset Maugham, or Mishima. Given the proper ingredients, the flat one-dimensional old wireless can cast a powerful spell.

At the risk of exposing a frivolous warp, I can't help but confess that my own particular favorite is BBC4's "Week Ending," an irreverent spoof based on current news events, many of which are so comic they needn't be run through a typewriter fitted with a funnybone.

Not all of "Week Ending" is drawn from the House of Parliament and the British trade union movement. An especially biting piece during the endless Watergate hullabaloo opened with a man intoning, in that Public Speaking IV fruitcake of a voice, "I, Richard Milhous Nixon, President of the United States, do solemnly swear that I will tell the truth, the whole truth, and nothing but the truth." In the brief silence that followed, a single laugh was heard, then another, and another, until the whole studio was filled with raucous, derisive ho-ho laughter at the mere suggestion.

Several weeks later, "Week Ending" reacted to the headlines about America's rogue warrior whose excessive combat zeal landed him in prison, from which he hoped to be sprung by means of a commuted sentence. "When Calley Comes Marching Home Again, Hurrah, Hurrah," sung to the old Civil War tune, reflected on the young lieutenant's valorous feat in running up a record body count of more than a hundred of what the radio spoof—and maybe Calley himself, for all I know—called wogs.

If and when the Deindorfer family ever comes marching home, as I expect we will for all the temptations to remain off-shore, my experiences on the consumer end of British radio and television will light the way while we pack. We'll include very few action replay clips from the telly, but we will run tapes of some of the marvelous BBC radio shows through Customs in case New York City airwaves are still polluted with the same big-beat all-news noises I keep trying to forget.

Chapter 10

The first time the home ec major in our family ever cooked a potful of a basic English ration known as runner beans, as part of what was otherwise a memorable feast celebrating the arrival of a vagabond young guest from Ardsley, New York, she thoughtlessly overlooked the necessity of shaving the whiskers off either side of each pod, which, while plainly her mistake, turned out to be my misfortune.

From the moment the vegetable dish went round the table events were preordained. If any one of us was to get a stray bean stringer caught in his throat—well, the outcome was predictable. Once it happened I went down the catalogue of home remedies, including a full crust of bread, with my usual good luck. The tenacious string remained lodged down in my windpipe somewhere, nothing dangerous, mind you, just enough to agitate me over the next two hours.

By ten o'clock it was clear that I'd better effect some optional plan such as a jiffy trip to the nearest hospital two miles away.

My condition remained satisfactory still, but given a terminal case of hypochondria, that bristling little doodad would feel the size of an anaconda once I got to bed, shut off the lights, and commenced to brood on the many morbid possibilities, one of them the fear that I surely wouldn't last out the night without strangling in my sleep.

At the hospital a nursing sister fed me several lozenges, which didn't score either, although they did taste better than the bread crust, and then rang up our family doctor, who, arriving fortified with enough instruments to embark on an appendix transplant, went foraging down the tunnel of my throat.

The fact that the doctor quickly managed to extract the remnant of that runner bean, along with the bulk of my dinner, isn't the point here. What gives the incident profound impact is the fact that the whole process—nurse, hospital casualty room, doctor coming in the night—cost me nothing at all. I was, as my family and I have been countless times before and since, the beneficiary of England's National Health Service, which our kindly pipe-smoking old American Medical Association forever vilifies for reasons that ought to be fairly obvious.

By way of contrast, that same freak accident would have run me or, with any luck, my Blue Cross—which generally has a Catch-22 specifically excluding whatever happens to beset me— a painful wallop back in fun city New York. It would have been $20 for the emergency room at Lenox Hill Hospital, $20 or $25 for any doctor willing to set foot into the perilous urban night provided the answering service could find one, and not much less in a less extravagant city the size of Aurora, Illinois, either.

Despite some defects, what the British call "The Scheme" amounts to such a roaring success throughout the country that more than 98 percent of the total population participates even though people can pay to see doctors on a private basis if they choose to. In communities like Wootton Bassett, Nottingham, Sodbury, Hereford, and Chipping Camden, the abundance of modern medicine is available to everyone at government expense.

"Everyone" specifically includes any tourists who just happen to be passing through at the time they come down with something or other. A Midwestern cousin of mine on a trip to London was much impressed by the treatment she received in the casualty ward of a London hospital after she was ambushed by a treacherous curb to the tune of a sprained ankle. "They even gave me a cane," she reported by telephone.

In discussing The Scheme with several American doctors, I found the one argument they have trouble refuting is the fact that, on the basis of every available study, the English are far healthier than ever before—and are, for that matter, healthier than Americans as a group, according to the most meaningful categories.

Of course, a comprehensive national health service isn't unique to England, or to Russia either, to mention a dread name the AMA regularly used to cite in an effort to raise everyone's blood pressure. State medicine exists in one form or another in Canada, France, West Germany, Italy, Switzerland, Australia, New Zealand, and the Scandinavian countries. Now that America finally has instituted government-subsidized medical care for older people I expect it won't be too long before a broader service is designed to cover everyone, whereupon those purists who insist on a private program can journey to see some masked doctor in the Outer Hebrides who beats a stick on a hollow log by way of asking the patient to say ahhh.

Yet the success of the English service in no way means that physicians, patients, and the bureaucracy assigned to administer it don't register some twanging complaints. They do. The criticism includes too little hospital space, slow treatment in surgical cases, insufficient wages for doctors, and the end of the so-called bedside manner. But the people list these and other defects with a constructive affection.

If not every last Englishman wants to stand drinks for the government-issue cures for dyspepsia, well, American bridegrooms aware of the alarming price levels back home actually have been known to hesitate in responding to that familiar "in sickness and in health" nuptial warranty. Among other things, the palsied old bedside manner isn't exactly a going concern in Dr. Kildare country any longer. It began fading out shortly after someone invented the telephone answering service, which enables an anonymous voice speaking on behalf of the regular G.P. to suggest you ring a standby, whose answering service then suggests you ring another standby, and so on, until any surviving member of the family can call the coroner, an eventuality that may have been very much in the cards all along, anyway, due to the leechcraft that sometimes passes for modern medicine in the United States.

My grumpy assessment goes beyond a badly set broken finger that won't ever straighten out again and a botched diagnosis—the medical equivalent of "pilot error"—on my septum, which deviates to a point where I'm able to breathe through only one nostril. Even at this distance it's difficult for me to consider American doctors without recalling to mind a local physician in the New England town where a professional football team I was doing time with had pitched its preseason training camp. When he volunteered his services as a spare doctor on a gratuitous basis, the coach figured why not. As an outsider the coach had no idea that prudent townspeople familiar with the doctor seldom let him treat them for anything more serious than acne. He was a cheery sort, and a great freak of a football fan, besides, but, sad to say, not much of a doctor.

During the first full-boom scrimmage it wasn't long before the first casualty, a linebacker, went down, grabbing hold of his knee and hollering. As the doctor picked up his satchel and hurried onto the field, several townspeople realized that the damaged player was in something of a double-jeopardy situation.

Finally, a young fan along the sidelines could restrain himself no longer. He thought it only good manners to warn the line-backer that what might look like a short, dumpy angel of mercy approaching wasn't necessarily so.

"Run, run, number fifty-four, get up and run," he bawled to the player still writhing on the ground, with the doctor almost upon him. "Run and save yourself before it's too late."

I wouldn't say that this Hippocratic disaster is typical, not with three practicing doctors in my own family, but I'm convinced he isn't exactly unique.

To be perfectly fair, I suspect that made-in-America doctors are entitled to a rather larger share of the world's goods, which they're clearly accumulating, than many of their fellow golfers. Even if their skill techniques aren't what they ought to be, medical school amounts to a major capital investment, doctors do put in brutally long hours, and annual country club dues have inflated like everything else, especially those monthly bills doctors run through the mails. Stateside doctors who fluoroscope a prospective patient's wallet as well as his rheumatic wishbone can't help but be skeptical. As *Medical Economics*—a publication so bulky, incidentally, that the mailman who delivers it might cough once or twice testing for a hernia every time he comes by —keeps reminding them in feverish case history articles, patients have been known to jump their bills before the mortician takes over.

Thanks to publications like *Medical Economics* as well as to their stock portfolios, affluent, hard-working U.S. doctors know they have a pretty good thing in capitalistic, free-enterprise medicine, and they look upon the government-sponsored system prevalent in England and elsewhere as a urine specimen. They're qualmish until the full lab report comes back. Meanwhile, meanwhile, the AMA's large percussion section continues its rackety paradiddles warning the American people—among them some 400,000 licensed doctors—that they've never had it so good.

If the skittish fears of typewriter-for-hire AMA propagandists are understandable, the fears of member doctors patently are not.

In case a comprehensive government medical system is ever enacted in Washington, the medical trade union would become largely redundant. But the doctors would remain far up the socioeconomic scale, in the upper 5 percent of individual earners whom the tax people take such a ferocious bite out of.

Even the existing order in our village of Lower Slaughter illustrates the realities. Guess who has the only private resident swimming pool? That same able and dedicated doctor also owns two cars, packs three children off to private—in the American sense of the word—schools, and holidays in France when his taste for snails comes to a boil.

While that swimming pool is something special, other doctor friends in the thrall of the National Health Service don't appear to be suffering any more than Dr. Glen Richmond back in Aurora, Illinois, who sometimes wonders if maybe St. Lucia wouldn't be more fun than Kingston. A pediatrician in Oxford admits to having the good life despite a fairly hellish office schedule; a young medical fishing companion owns a magnificent pile of a Georgian home in nearby Guiting Power; another friend on the Welsh border is so comfortably fixed he's investing in livestock as a tax shelter.

Those and other acquaintances seem in no way the exception to a familiar pattern in both England and America. One evening after I flogged the River Itchen in Hampshire for brown trout with the usual success, meaning not very much, I decided to treat myself to a dinner at the Sheriff Hotel in Stockbridge, whose kitchen I regard as one of the most distinguished in all of England. As I wheeled our old banger of a car up to the hotel for a memorable and justifiably expensive feed I couldn't help but notice that the parking lot looked like a Jaguar showroom except for the convertible Bentley proudly standing near the door.

"Where do all the gastronomes come from?" I asked the chef's son.

"Winchester, Southampton, London, lots of places."

"What kind of people?" I inquired, regarding a number of well-tailored clients seated in the small dining room.

"Different sorts, but we get quite a few doctors, many from London."

"Oh."

In the first year of our sabbatical my family wore a groove in the road to the private-pool doctor's surgery, which is to say office, two miles away in Bourton-on-the-Water. Joan suffered a badly sprained ankle, an eye infection, a lingering case of bronchitis, and a gash requiring a series of three tetanus shots. I had trouble with a treacherous knee cartilage, the runner bean caper, a severe sinus infection, a variant dry rot spelled pityriasis rosea, and a high-fever virus. Our bike-riding, tree-climbing son had the usual aches and pains, infected tonsils, two heavy colds, and a virus, not to mention allergy shots he needed regularly every second week, which, if they hurt him just as much as ever, are $10 a pop less painful to me.

The year-end medical inventory might sound excessive even at a meeting of Hypochondriacs Anonymous, I suspect, but it's fairly routine for the snakebitten Deindorfer family. Altogether we must have made a total of fifty trips into the surgery, several times on what amounted to a group basis. Altogether we paid the doctor a total of nothing, absolutely nothing, zip, aside from prescription medicines, which we consumed like popcorn and which ran us merely 20 pence, 50¢ U.S., per prescription form no matter how exotic the mycin family pharmaceuticals involved.

Even now I remember the day I toddled into the surgery complaining of a mild fever and the attendant trimmings. After the regular preliminaries with a wooden tongue depressor, the blood pressure gauge, and the tap, tap, tapping up and down my spinal chord, the doctor prescribed a supply of some new wonder drug, big as horse pills, four every day for a full week, which ran me the standard 20 pence, although a couple of juju men on the corner of Lexington Avenue and Seventy-first Street in New York City I know would have hit me at least $10 for the goods without so much as blushing.

Like so much else in life, however, that nominal prescription charge is the subject of considerable heat among native English patients. "That's a good bit to pay for *me* serum, twenty pee, another twenty pee every month or so," a dear lady who obviously hasn't ever done any marketing on Lexington Avenue sourly told my wife during a catch-as-catch-can discussion on The Scheme.

Residents who consider the piddling incidental cost exorbitant need only follow the lead of a neighbor so impressively stalwart I can't help but think he wasn't born so much as he was quarried. He avoids prescription fees by avoiding the doctors entitled to write them. This amiable widower allowed that a visit he'd paid the doctor the day before represented a major news event.

"Yup, last time I saw the doctor was thirty-two years ago come July, still remember it, I do, a carbuncle, nasty one, too," he told me, citing chapter and verse in case I had any doubts.

England's state dentistry isn't as simple as the medicine, or as gratuitous, but it also has its advantages, especially for one who suffered the full periodontal course in New York City several years ago. I wasn't able to sort out the structure of this offshoot government-issue system until I stopped by the office of a dentist for my first English curettage and scaling.

On lowering myself into his chair and opening wide I was scraped in much the same way I've grown accustomed to at home, although my American connection—among periodontists he's looked on as a periodontist's periodontist—is probably more proficient because he treats only patients who've literally gone long in the tooth. Still, the price differential was substantial. In my case I paid two pounds, or $5 U.S., instead of the usual $30. Several weeks later, my wife was dunned merely three pounds, or $7.50 U.S., for X-rays, drilling, and a new inlay requiring two appointments.

My only quibble with the oral hygiene I submit to on a quarterly basis is strictly an incidental one. My dentist happens to be left-handed. Even after more than a year I haven't got used to being treated from what seems, after a long career wearing a plastic bib, the offside. But my reaction is as nothing compared with the psychodrama that a bouncy, effervescent friend, Jean Steward, who has her teeth done at the same address, took part in. Since Mrs. Steward seldom stops talking, in or out of the dental chair, it wasn't surprising that she was in full voice the morning our mutual dentist moved in from behind her with a long harpoon of a needle containing the usual anesthesia. Still talking, not yet accustomed to the sponsor's blind-side approach, a bit edgy because she didn't relish the prospect of the drilling soon to commence, anyway, she nervously flung out her left hand at the worst possible moment. All of a sudden her hand was impaled on the needle, which pumped in enough batwing extract to turn it numb right up to the fingernails.

"It couldn't have been any worse," Mrs. Steward informed a visitor later.

"Yes it could," he said after considering. "As long as your hand was anesthetized, he might have extracted a finger. No sense wasting the stuff, right."

In the last few years England has finally embarked on a major campaign encouraging natives to hold onto their birthright teeth. Newspapers, radio, and television features, pamphlets, posters, placards, and school lectures at the village level all stress the importance of using a toothbrush, visiting the dentist regularly, and scaling down the sweets and jelly carbohydrates that sustain too many people. On returning home from a shock-and-alarm school lecture one afternoon our son volunteered an eventful tribute to the impact of the campaign. "I'm not buying any more of those big Milky Way bars," he announced, but it wasn't long before he backslid.

High technology has come to England too, dental floss, electric toothbrushes, even high-pressure water-pics, the latter only now beginning to catch hold in London and other large urban areas. If fluoridating the water has not been put into effect in most places, it's because medical authorities are still not convinced there's more good than harm to it.

What's probably more effective than anything else, however, is a tremendous new emphasis on preventive rather than corrective dentistry so routine in years gone by. More and more youngsters are having their teeth straightened, for example, and adults who automatically used to have a defective tooth pulled now submit to inlays and bridgework.

As a conservation-oriented bloke determined to hang onto my own teeth at any cost—any cost added up to $480 in the case of one mutinous tusk preserved in at least a technical sense thanks to endless drilling and impressions, three visits to a New York City root canal specialist, and a crown big enough for the former King Zog of Albania—I'm impressed to see the preventive concept accelerating throughout England despite a certain amount of resistance. After learning that I was suffering a minor toothache, origin not yet determined, a status quo neighbor offered up the predictable old advice: "Have it out."

On the basis of a previous conversation on the same general theme, my reaction was hardly one of surprise. As our neighbor related the story, she was seventeen when her dentist informed her he'd have to administer gas because the normal injection of anesthesia hadn't effectively put out the lights in her upper left side where he planned to extract a total of one tooth.

"If you have to do that you might just as well take out the lot," she said, and he did.

No-nonsense logic like that helps explain why the deafening new information campaign seems a very wise move. Even today more than one-third of the entire population over age sixteen has no teeth they can call their own. Maybe the soft English boiled dinner isn't really a matter of taste.

For what it's worth, long before I had a close-up look for myself, I was aware of the fact that millions of Englishmen have teeth—provided they have teeth, that is—no brighter than local weather conditions. My father, a practicing dentist for almost fifty years, occasionally used to comment on the situation from his vantage point in Illinois. During a television variety program one evening I remember him sadly shaking his head when a renowned young British singer opened her mouth to reveal something more than a lovely lyric voice.

"My god, boy," he rasped, "twenty years old—and a full upper plate."

Eyeglasses as well as proxy teeth come under the benevolent umbrella of the National Health Service too, else prudent Englishmen wouldn't all be wearing almost identical government-issue horn frames. But anyone so careless as to break the frame or the glass is on his own. I learned that for myself on splintering one lens of the American spectacles I wear to distinguish day from night at much over ten feet. An oculist named Hardcastle Williams in Stow-on-the-Wold ran me up a replacement for just two pounds, or $4.80 U.S., about half what Charles Skolnick used to bill me when things went hazy back home.

But the difference in native medicine as it's practiced in England and the United States can best be seen by considering two real-life experiences. Some time ago a Britisher taken ill during a visit to New York City was rushed to the hospital where he died ten days later despite commendable efforts of some good doctors and nurses. His widow was presented, along with his watch and other effects, a bill that came to just over $12,000.

At approximately that same time an American youngster touring the English backlands with his parents was rushed to a hospital in Cheltenham seriously dehydrated because of a lingering virus. Intravenous feeding and a series of tests began while the parents stayed in a private room and were themselves fed three times a day in a small dining room. Four days in the hospital, tests, lab fees, doctors and private nurses, and private rooms for both the boy and his parents came to a total—repeat, total—of exactly three pounds, ten pence, or $7.45 U.S. As the hospital supervisor apologetically explained, the three pounds, 10 pence covered the bland but perfectly adequate meals the two adults had consumed, which regrettably are not part of the dole.

Memories of the ailing youngster being restored to bouncy good health can't help but stay with me. After all, the worried father there was someone I'm all too familiar with. Me.

Chapter 11

Several summers ago, an American was asked just what she did at a tumbledown weekend shack in Claryville, New York, while her husband was out fishing the Neversink River with rather more ardor than success. She considered the question briefly. "What do I do?" she repeated. "Why, nothing—nothing at all. That's what makes it so pleasant."

In a literal sense the answer wasn't altogether accurate, of course, but at least it was accurate in the context of the by-the-numbers golf, tennis, and mambo lessons the other woman was accustomed to. Personally, our liberated friend lazed away her country weekends picking wildflowers, potting around the country for antiques, reading cloak-and-dagger paperbacks, swimming the river her husband so hopefully flogged with his fly rod, curling up for a nap on the back lawn.

Not long after Joan and I settled in England we realized that Dorothy Roberts of Ardsley and Claryville, New York, would approve of the native approach to leisure, which is informal, to say the least. In Slaughter and Lower Swell, Northleach and Milton-under-Wychwood, descendants of the Industrial Revolution have raised doing not much to the level of an art form. The torpid pace couldn't suit us more.

For what it's worth, the easy pace isn't confined to smaller villages standing in the Cotswolds, or on the Devon coast, or up in the misty Yorkshire moors. The normal pace in London is usually less frantic than it is in New York City despite the fact that both urban sprawls have approximately the same population. Only more qualified observers can relate this constrained life style to the dramatically lower incidence of ulcers, respiratory infections, mental disorders, divorce, heart attacks, and other stress-related problems in London, but I have my own suspicions.

Wherever they happen to dwell, most of the English people have a lovely sense of leisure. In their spare time they garden; they indulge in what they call liedowns, or naps; they read newspapers, magazines, and books in great gulps. If the contemporary literature they feed on isn't all that it might be—a classic Player seated near me in a café one morning was pop-eyed tracking the pages of something entitled *Confessions of a Kinky Teeny Bopper*— the English nevertheless buy almost three times as many books as Americans on a per capita basis.

On weekends and over the summer holidays, troops of people like to get out into the speckled green countryside. Often they set off on aimless pleasure-bent trips bound nowhere in particular. Even after our Arab brethren sent the price of petrol up to more than the price of beer, the English continue to embark on the sort of random Sunday drives my own family used to indulge in in the thirties, when we'd follow back roads through Sugar Grove, Lily Lake, Bald Mound, and, with any luck, maybe even a Burlington streamliner highballing over the flat Midwestern land.

One day Joan, Scott, a neighborhood youngster, and I scheduled a trip without any fixed destination in the hopes we might encounter something more than fields ripening for harvest. We reached a rural junction just as a fleet of old Rolls-Royce cars came by, stately old schooners sailing over rolls of green land. There were nine of them, including what looked like a Phantom II 40–50 Continental, circa 1931, light yellow, in mint condition. On the off chance a vintage radiator might boil over and we could have a close-up look at the cars, we joined up for a lovely twenty-mile tour through Clapton-on-Hill, Sherborne, the Barringtons, and, finally, Burford, where our own relatively new radiator erupted and forced us to give up the chase.

An essential part of the familiar English motoring trips are the rest stops along the way, which are frequent. All they need is a formal layby, a clearing, an open field along the road, something big enough for a family sprawl. Out of the trunk of the car come folding chairs and a table, a basket of plates, cups, and utensils, sacks of sandwiches, meat pies, cheese, crisps, tomatoes, fruit, cakes, and thermos jugs. Many also carry tea kettles and sterno stoves with a lot of mileage on them, which are useful for standard tea breaks around eleven in the morning and in late afternoon, when layby areas tend to become so clogged with vehicles that innocent visiting Americans driving past probably mark it off as a ten-car collision.

These casual motorists frequently put deck chairs and blankets to even better use once their ample feeding is finished. I counted sixteen people napping—or at least completely motionless—one noon hour in Slaughter. A fellow about my own age, with a loaf of bread, a wheel of cheese, and a plastic bowl of apples and bananas on a table right next to him, was asleep when I did my body count. From the looks of things, such as the provisions, which hadn't diminished any, he hadn't moved a muscle by the time I returned at four o'clock.

Local weather conditions being what they are, subject to change, it isn't surprising that Britishers who enjoy warming their bones in a layby or along a stream like the River Eye twining through Slaughter take advantage of good weather at night as well. Conveyed by campers, caravans, bikes, motorcycles, and sometimes nothing more than their own feet, they go into the country looking for a meadow or field on which they can unfurl a tent. A bouncy man encamped near Bourton told me he'd been camping out on summer weekends for most of his eighty-three years, although two grandchildren kept warning him to slow down.

"I tell them what I tell you, it's what keeps me young, it does, camping and the odd pint at a near pub," he said in a voice that implied he wouldn't mind. At the near pub I walked him to the odd pint soon multiplied to three.

But unscheduled drives, casual trips, and weekend tenting in no way cover the whole grass-roots English scene. The landscape is covered with walkers, too, solitary or packs of club walkers, clad in heavy hiking boots with raincoats strapped to their backs. They are vigorous men and women of all ages, with ruddy turn-verein glows to their faces, who swing canes or notched shoulder-high thumbsticks that give the owners good service as they climb angles in the land.

Weather conditions, distance, and even time of year are less important to the more fervent hikers than the elemental urge to get some ground under their feet. On what amounted to a very cold December day by English standards, more than two dozen members of the Ramblers Club of Cheltenham, sixteen miles away, came clumping through Slaughter on a satisfying back-to-nature hike. Bird watchers, brass-rubbers, amateur painters, photo clubs, knockabout nature groups, and bell-ringers rove the land in pursuit of their own pleasures, too. The bell-ringers are intruiging. Their estimated numbers run as high as 50,000, and they're as familiar as bats up in church steeples where they pull for hours, driven by visions of achieving a Double Bob Major, a Canterbury Surprise, a Grandsire Triple, or some other especially prodigious peal. "Mad, very mad, the bell-ringers are mad as they come," a leathery man I know said just before he organized an annual football match in the local river.

The comfortable shadow of Izaak Walton still shows on

streams, quarries, and lakes throughout the United Kingdom. Game fishermen cast for trout, sea trout, and salmon; coarse fishermen rig ledger bait lines for chub, tench, and pike. If an ichthyologist's tastes are as catholic as mine, he can fish right round the calendar. That wasn't a partridge in a pear tree on the eighth day of Christmas in 1973, for example. It was a Number 16 Blue Dun Nymph fly I'd been casting for grayling in the River Dickler near Bourton before a myopic back cast hung me in the pear tree. Although I fished at no particular profit during the Christmas season despite several intriguing rises, it was nice to be able to fish for anything at all after the trout season shut down. By the time an itinerant angler realizes that a pound or pound-and-a-half grayling is hellish hard to catch, the salmon have begun again late in January on the River Wye in Wales where silvery sea-run fish aren't the only competition for law-abiding visitors.

Despite a number of rival claims, the Wye appears to attract the most enterprising poachers in all of Wales, which amounts to a walloping tribute. Even in a country celebrated for its poachers—an adage has it that "The Scotsman poaches because he's a poacher; the Welshman poaches because he's a Welshman"—locals seem to be in a class by themselves. After dark, hardy sinners go out for salmon with gaffs, spears, pitchforks, nets, seines, snags, wires, traps, snorkels, poison, dynamite, and occasionally their bare hands. They use everything from worms to salmon-roe paste as bait, and they land fish of fifty pounds and more without making the local papers, unless they get caught. One resourceful old-timer occasionally goes to the trouble of staging a bogus diversionary raid. He has an accomplice set off an explosion two or three miles up the Wye, waits while policemen, river watchers, and landowners rush into the Welsh night in search of illegal fishermen, and then quietly throws his net across a narrow neck of water with no interference.

"The ones who do the poaching are nice chaps, most of them, the same as anyone else," a voluble newsdealer in Hay-on-Wye once told me. "You can't blame them for taking an odd fish. After all, very few locals haven't had a fresh salmon one way or another."

One local who admitted to having his share of fresh Wye salmon was Percivale Price, a brisk, bouncy, thoroughly likable construction man. Price has been fishing almost as long as he can remember for salmon, trout, and pike—"legal now and then too," he likes to remind skeptics, proudly showing a worn, outdated license as evidence. Like many friends and neighbors, Price doesn't restrict himself to rod and reel. "I shot an eighteen-pound salmon with a gun," he told me. "I must have taken two pounds out of the neck where I shot it. But, oh my, we certainly ate salmon. We ate fresh salmon for breakfast, lunch, tea, and dinner. We even got up in the night to eat fresh salmon."

More controversial blood sports are so profuse they put a real dent in the Natural Selection factor, only don't put it that way to devotees else they'll bore a hole straight through you with one of those you-blinking-bleeding-heart looks. They shoot pheasant, duck, quail, and small game; they set greyhounds to coursing for rabbit, beagles to snuffling for hare, and bloodhounds to mucking riverland for otter, and everywhere follow the unspeakable ride to hounds in pursuit of the inedible. Some of the regular fox hunts are considered better than others. Our own Heythrop Hunt is so well regarded that real-estate advertisements for Cotswold properties in the national newspapers often cite it as part of the sales pitch, like apartment ads in Manhattan used to include a Public School 6 reference.

On strictly an aesthetic plane a proper hunt is unashamedly gorgeous to behold. Down a steep hillside they come, riders dressed in formal red or black, whippers-in dressed in regulation green, as many as two hundred horses, perhaps eighteen pair of hounds—they're always called hounds, incidentally, never dogs —on the trail of a raggedy fox, the huntmaster's horn a crisp peal in the day, the banshee wail of the hounds a sort of music all its own, the whole scene straight off an old print. The hunt often develops into a chase between not only hounds and a target fox but also between the hunt itself and onlookers like myself who drive back roads in breakneck attempts to see what we can.

One Saturday morning, a splendid old fellow voyeur in plus fours, a tweed jacket, and a grouse helmet took me in hand as we followed the hunt along a dry wall near Upper Swell. "The wind is all wrong for the hounds; dodgy, very dodgy, shifting about, isn't it?" he said. He swung his binoculars left to right and offered further technical commentary. "This isn't the best pack in the country, either, no matter what they say about Heythrop; overfed, some of them; too many not really blooded, either. Look at that now. They're onto a false scent." The old boy's voice rose to a shout although the hounds and hunters were well out of earshot.

In the end I heard they got the fox they'd lost scent of that morning, or a fox answering the same general description, anyway, but I was long gone, back home again, having seen the colorful part of the hunt without having to watch the hateful denouement. I expect I'm a lot like my father when it comes to the prospect of unnecessary blood. Back when he was a student in Chicago he attended his first professional wrestling match, which he thought was stimulating up to the moment—a high point in the choreography the principals undoubtedly worked out in the dressing room earlier—one of them got a wicked-looking hold on the other's wishbone and loudly threatened to break his elbow if he didn't give up. It seemed so genuine that my father went queasy and promptly bolted the arena.

If fox hunting is a lovely spectator sport up to a point, it can also be fairly hazardous for participants. Blood must be spilt on a hunt, it is said, and the blood occasionally is that of the fox. Until a lady I knew only by sight plucked at my arm and initiated a brief dialogue in a specialty food store we were both picking clean late in the season our first year, however, I wasn't aware of how very dangerous it could be.

"Oh, thank goodness it wasn't you," she said.

"How's that?"

"Thank goodness it wasn't you. When I heard an American riding with Heythrop was killed last week I thought it might be you."

Our weekly newspaper confirmed the tragic fact that the dear thing hadn't been exaggerating, although I had to track through fourteen inches of type describing the hunt in infinite detail—"the fox took a left-handed turn in the kale above Blackpits, thence afoot in Snow Bottom to try the hole at Shadington and race over Woeful Lake"—before I found the news squeezed into six lines of type: "The day ended sadly as Mr. Paul Rettig, a good sportsman from California who was over here for the winter's hunting, had a fatal fall." But the gummy mystique of what is basically a pretty sport eludes me still. In a subsequent issue of *Horse and Hound,* an anonymous contributor to the obituary column suggested that the victim's family could be consoled by the fact that the hounds were running well at the time the accident occurred.

The sprawling realities of the blood sports ought not obscure an important accompanying aspect of the British leisure scene. It is filled with more conventional competitive participant sports, too. Men, women, and children knock the stuffing out of tennis balls and play proper badminton indoors during the winter. Tormented blokes golf whatever the weather, including a foursome we spotted at Burford on Christmas Day, just like Mr. Ludolph, who used to hit a red ball in the snowbanks in Aurora, Illinois.

In the villages kids engage in pickup versions of what, on other fields in other times, amount to England's major spectator sports: soccer, a wildly exciting nonstop game as the First Division professionals play it; rugby, a less barbarous brand of American football without protective padding; and cricket, slow, graceful, every bit as exciting as watching turnips grow. In season spectators are also treated to horse racing, motor racing, championship golf and tennis, sculling and canoe racing, track and field, prizefighting, and what the billboards invariably describe as All-

Star International Wrestling, such as a headline match between the Mighty Bald-Headed Assassin and the Wildman of Borneo ("Half Man, Half Animal—Must Be Seen").

The wide range of spectator sports offers the British the chance to indulge in a sellout participant sport of their own—betting. Natives bet on practically anything. In response to numerous inquiries from clients who had the fever, Ladbrokes, one of the big licensed bookies, several of which fatten up selling weekly football pools, actually put a price on the prospects to fill the vacant Archbishop of Canterbury primacy a few months after our arrival. They quoted the Most Reverend Donald Coggan as a three-to-one favorite and, sure enough, Coggan won going away.

Few villages are so small they can't support a betting parlor for hopeful locals who want to put money on the horses. I wasn't certain a retired Player who lives a few cottages away in Lower Slaughter had any interests beyond working the kitchen garden whose produce wins him blue ribbons in the annual competition until I saw a familiar bike leaning against Thomas Henry Bey Limited in next-door Bourton. Predictably, bingo is popular as orange squash. A resourceful addict who doesn't mind traveling a few miles can find a bingo game every night of the week without embracing the Catholic faith.

Given the assorted speculation available in our bucolic area, even a righteous moralist generally standing foursquare against such things has been known to lapse. Every Monday night I contribute my 15 pence, or 37¢ U.S., to the vendor who collects for the soccer pool. I've won a total of only two pounds, or $5 U.S., since I acquired the habit, but I did far better when, only a few weeks before Nixon's forced resignation, Ladbrokes put an official even-money price on the president completing his full term of office. The bread I cast upon the waters returned 10 pounds sterling, or $25 U.S., which I contributed to our Village Hall Committee to underwrite repairs on an antique clock. Easy come, easy go.

At the risk of offending real high-rollers who look down on such mechanical diversions, I must also confess that among the fixtures in our kitchen is a working slot machine we occasionally spin while a prime joint of meat is stewing in its juices. It's a classic old model by Mills of Chicago and we picked it up in an antique shop in Cheltenham for 12 pounds, or $30 U.S., which struck me as a nifty buy even before we opened it up and found six pounds, or $15, in six-pence pieces the antique-monger surprisingly had overlooked. I wonder what price Ladbrokes would put on *that* happening again.

Despite the ample supply of native fun and games, however, the English sporting scene lacks one essential ingredient. Personally, I'm a certified football freak. Anyone who questions the fact need only consider the evidence: season tickets, three sets of them, Giants, Jets, and West Point; a transistor radio fitted with earplugs, seven-by-fifty Leitz binoculars, a television set back in New York City that starts doing calisthenics around nine o'clock on Monday nights; and a memory that, although leaky on matters considered significant in our split-level culture, is perfectly sound when it comes to recollecting essential data like the starting backfield for the College All-Stars in their game with the Chicago Bears in 1936 (Miller Munjas, Al Nichelini, Bill Shepard, and Beattie Feathers).

Soon after we settled in the Cotswolds that first year I bleakly realized it was going to be fourth down and three thousand miles to go for me right through to the Superbowl. The international edition of the *Herald Tribune*, our only daily link with the paleoliths running square-out patterns back home, chose to ignore or grudgingly carry only line score of all those preseason exhibitions I customarily feed on by way of conditioning myself for official league games to follow. On what I knew to be the first full Saturday of college football, things reached such a point that I phoned the London bureau of the *New York Times* to get the results, but with no success. For a terminal case conditioned to tracking results of games out to Long Beach and Weber State fairly early on Saturday nights, it was a long wait for the Monday *Herald Tribune.*

Briefly, all too briefly, I thought that so far from it all I hit on a mother lode late one night that first September. Trying to dial in a newscast on the radio, my eardrums suddenly warmed to the flat, faintly hysterical sound of a play-by-play of the Nebraska-UCLA game—brass bands audible in the background, the whole thing courtesy of the Armed Forces Network.

But just as Nebraska got to moving upfield another voice, thick and menacing, came through, faintly at first, then louder and louder, until the game was completely blotted out, to return only intermittently the rest of the night. In an intrigue-flavored era of superpowers I idly wondered if the anonymous Russian voice wasn't part of some devilish Soviet ruse to jam Armed Forces Radio and deprive American troopers manning the lonely outposts of freedom their morale-building downhome football.

The only game the rest of the season that was audible throughout was a Giant-Raider gasser from Oakland; the final score was Raiders 42, Giants 0, or not what you'd call competitive despite the breathless efforts of two monotones sharing the microphone. On the other hand, a stirring Steeler-Denver showdown had my nerve ends twanging like old times before that alien basso horned in for another few pages of Chekhov in the mother tongue.

With electronics so spotty, I sent up a flare for help to friends back in New York, who responded properly by airmailing me sports sections of the *Times,* Sunday sections to cover the collegiate scene, Monday to cover the real stuff. Soon an unexpected and more convenient means of slaking my thirst opened up.

As I was driving away from the U.S. Air Force base at Upper Heyford, after gathering some background for a magazine article I'd been assigned, a lovely leathery noise rose in the air. I braked to a stop. Over a rise in the land, on a striped field fitted with regulation goal posts at either end, about fifty servicemen were practicing football under the command of a coach. He was built along the usual lines—that is, he didn't have any neck to speak

127

of and his shoulders ran right up to his earlobes. Watching the squad work out that afternoon I realized I missed the grand old game even more than I'd suspected. It's nearness, not absence, that makes the heart grow fonder.

Every Saturday that the Skyking service champs played home games there I was, perched on a wooden seat around the forty-yard line, yelling my head off. If the artistic level wasn't all I'd hoped, a live draw play is a draw play is a draw play—and besides, I managed to fill in a couple of other evocative tastes too, thanks to vendors peddling root beer and barbecued spareribs, while the Americans' cars in the parking lot and the American accents round me contributed to the spell.

One Saturday I got to yarning with an effervescent black enlisted man seated in front of me whose technical grasp of the game was, to put it charitably, minimal, although he was, like television sports commentators at home, fairly good at incidental detail such as the opposition's won-lost record and the college team, if any, that financed the higher education of some whopping tackle before he went straight and joined up. "The thing about that flankerback, he don't do nothing right," he remarked after the object of his scorn dropped another pass, his syntax such an echo of what I used to hear during my years of residence in Section 52 at Yankee Stadium that I almost choked.

About halfway through my first season so far from home I uncovered another bonanza, the Playboy Club on Park Lane in London, which caters to third-and-long nuts every Tuesday, Wednesday, and Thursday. Except for the ornamental indoor ambience, the pregame ritual struck me as appropriate on my very first visit. Indentured bunnies, all plastic smiles and dorsal fins, fetched drinks; itinerants beyond the range of Yale Bowl, Shea Stadium, and Channel 2 exchanged banal shoptalk ("Nobody could pump fake like Johnny U"); buffet tables were piled high with hams, hot dogs, hamburgers, cole slaw, and sliced tomatoes.

Once the film began I went into my usual trance. There they

were, padded mesomorphs so big they nearly blotted out the screen, Mean Joe Greene and Dave Hampton, Franco Harris and Roman Gabriel, rich gladiators with thick legs and defective knee cartilages, the traditional sights and sounds, including an obvious holding penalty by number 62 the official missed. The color film showed only highlights of two games played nine days earlier, of course, but it was football, copyrighted American football, and the old juices started running again.

Ever since that memorable discovery the bunnies have seen a good bit of me in season, although perhaps not quite as much as they'd like. Once a week I confect some taffy about urgent business in the city, fold the latest *Herald Tribune* in my pocket, and catch the train for London an hour and forty minutes away. Toward the end of the season I stop by the front desk for an important word with Playboy management. Management agrees to mail me a full schedule for next season, showing exact times and dates for films of college bowl games, the complicated pro playoffs, and the Superbowl.

I'm all for the British putting their spare time to admirable use picnicking, hiking, riding to hounds, falling asleep, tracking cricket. But a thwarted football freak doing time in England straight through the season can't afford any busted signals, can he?

Chapter 12

Back in a simpler, gentler age my brother Jack and I frequently used to get away from it all by investing a dime for an afternoon of pure gingerbread at the Tivoli Theater in Aurora, Illinois, where a cadaverous impresario supplemented the standard ration of cowpoke shoot-outs with just enough romantic comedies to offer us a faint glimmer of another life out beyond the Fox River Valley.

My mind's eye still goes red recapturing the basic ingredients of those vintage old romances—a cupcake of a career girl in a dazzling apartment in Manhattan or maybe Beverly Hills; a male lead all padded shoulders, slicked-down hair, and convertible Packard; a madcap round of night clubs staging floor shows approximately the size of the Tournament of Roses parade. But being young and wonderfully innocent—it seemed impossible to be one without being the other in Aurora in the nineteen thirties —we swallowed it all, along with taffy apples we'd prudently packed in from the Theodore Brothers' candy store next door.

For all our feckless naïveté, however, one fixed scene sure to appear as the film unwound invariably struck the two of us as absurd make-believe. Sooner or later, sometimes relevant to what passed as the story line, sometimes not, one of the mummers, generally that fellow with the Packard, casually picked up a telephone and casually dialed a number. In a nonchalant sort of way he'd whirl the dial once, twice, three, four, five, six, even seven times.

At around the fifth or sixth spin, Jack and I used to smile, nudge one another and exchange scolding come-come looks. We knew for a fact that phone numbers consisted of merely four figures, like our 6097 home phone and our father's 5657 office phone. Even allowing for the fact that Manhattan or Los Angeles had more telephones than Aurora, population 47,600 at the time, nobody had a number running six or seven digits, and Hollywood, whose produce we otherwise applauded, couldn't put one over on us.

Well, Jack, here I am, in a village of 191 people with phone number 3045120958.

The fact that we happen to have a phone at all—"We're on the phone," the English say in announcing the miracle of installation —is intoxicating. After first filing our official application and arranging for a phone company engineer to come for an inspection visit, we waited just over a year, during which time we poached calls at a neighbor's house or else shuffled two hundred yards up the road to the coin box. What you do in an English coin box is dial the number first, listen to the rings, and, once successful contact has been established, with the other party actually audible on the line, press a 2-pence piece into the slot at the sound of some threatening pip-pips.

Like so much else in the United Kingdom, however, standard phone technique has to allow for some regional variations, such as Wales where I kept dialing what I knew to be a perfectly accurate number with no results beyond a mechanical strangling sound, until a serving wench in the lodge where I was stopping mercifully explained the local ground rules. In Wales you invest —to use the word in its classic sense, since the phone sometimes ingests the coin without producing a call—the 2 pence before, not after, ringing the number.

If the telephone is different from what we were accustomed to back where folksy old Ma Bell used to unplug my conversations in mid-sentence, so is the going rate. As mentioned, local calls from a box run two English pence, or 5¢ U.S., and long-distance calls, with the same system of discount rates after six at night and over the weekends, come to about half our price.

The memory of the notable day our own phone finally was installed remains locked in my mind. All too early one morning booming artillery shells began erupting somewhere close by. Predictably, the noise attracted several resident youngsters, among them, just as predictably, our own, who went whooping into the dawn clad in the pajamas everyone ought to be wearing at that hour. From our bedroom window I focused one red eye on a working shovel digger, a snorkel truck boosting a laborer onto a neighboring rooftop, two phone trucks, and a total of nine men. On the basis of previous close-up encounters with British industry, I managed to blot out the suspicion that a picked work gang was running up a ten-room house from scratch.

With the digger supplying fortissimo background music, the high-wire performer hammered on the rooftop, two colleagues in bib overalls strung a line over the stream, a technician fitted brackets up under the eaves of another neighbor's house, and reserve employees humped ladders back and forth and littered the area with cigarette ends. The elaborate drama unfolded in the normal leisurely manner, which was fine with the children, who hadn't had much excitement since Quentin the Poacher fell in the stream several days before. Just when it seemed the lines actually were to be run into our cottage, the whole crew suddenly melted away to a green across from the manor house for a jolly old tea break consisting largely of cold sausage rolls and orange squash. I'd rashly promised to make several business calls before lunch, on what I assumed would be our very own phone. But the fact that the English don't perform with the sullen efficiency of installation technicians in New York City left me no alternative. Up the familiar track to the coin box I went, hidey-ho, jingling a pocketful of two-pence pieces, there to win a few and lose a few, the error factor being what it is.

By mid-afternoon a basic black phone finally stood on the edge of the oak bookshelves in our lounge. Total elapsed work time: five hours, thirty-eight minutes. Once the work gang drove away in the snorkel, the digger, and the two vans, thereby diminishing the resident population by approximately half, a genial, equally casual management representative arrived for an ABC on how to use the new phone. It wasn't so much a matter of the dial, which goes clockwise same as the U.S. model, or the long numbers, which frequently demand the finger strength of a trap drummer.

"You'll be needing this, won't you?" he said.

"Yes, indeed," I replied. "Only I wish we didn't."

With that the phonemonger treated us to a red directory in which STD area codes appear in small eyestrain print. To my wife's despair—she had done little time in the coin box the previous year, that burden being defined, by a vote of one-to-one, as strictly a masculine responsibility, like washing the dishes—STD codes vary right down to the village level. Whereas we used to use catch-all area code 312 to establish contact with friends and relatives anywhere in grass-roots northern Illinois, for instance, every community in the United Kingdom has its own specific numbered code. Chipping Norton is 383, Nottingham 0602, Wotton-under-Edge 045 385.

What makes the STD system more frustrating still is the fact that code numbers are frequently revised, which means that our directory resembles an old high school composition after it has undergone the wanton editorial pencil of an English teacher. Invariably, I suppose, the wave of the future being what it is, revised STD numbers are longer than those they replace. STD 922 now reads STD 9922. In view of all the chicken tracks that sully our directory, something more than my bifocals stand alongside our victory telephone. We keep a five-inch magnifying glass as well.

When the management representative concluded his droning spiel on ways and means, it was plainly time for my first practice call. I rang a friend in our own STD range, dialing only five numbers instead of nine or ten. Faintly, very faintly, talking through a layer of backfire, my friend replied, whereupon I cast a golden line: "What hath these motherhuggers wrought now?"

Since that scratchy first helping of 3045120958, my eardrums have grown accustomed to the sound of static or, perhaps even worse, no sound at all. Periodically, England's telephone system issues an official report boasting of impressive improvements, but I know better. If the government-issue system accurately reflects the technical glories of socialism, the John Birch Society might just as well add me to the mailing list.

Life is a matter of timing, Napoleon is reported to have said —timing and a reliable phone connection. All too often in my experience jackhammer noises commence or the line goes dead at the worst possible moment.

An especially despairing example unfolded the afternoon a magazine editor rang me from New York City to ask whether I'd embark on an intriguing article assignment. Of course I would. Before I got around to posing the Big Question I eloquently painted an extravagant scenario of all the research, the travel, the time, and the effort required for such a challenging assignment. Since the editor emitted sympathetic clucking sounds during my recital I was convinced that I'd reached the psychological moment where I could hit him for $1,250 instead of my standard $1,000 fee.

In the favorable circumstances so persuasively created, the phone suddenly went dead. I rang the overseas operator begging her to reestablish contact. After exploring the prospects, she politely explained that the transatlantic lines to America not only were engaged but calls were backed up for another two hours.

Any wistful hope of recapturing that magical consumer-oriented moment with a quick followthrough letter along the same lines was clearly doomed, if only because my typewriter isn't fitted with a key to produce the catch in my throat. Subsequently, I researched and wrote the piece at the same old coolie wage. It's a great pity an injured party can't sue the phone service for infidelity.

English calls often include background noises straight out of the stove works, don't ring at all, or startle some stranger in, say, Steeple Astin instead of London, but those and other adversities are nothing to me. In New York City the system is, if anything, even more comical, despite far higher rates, starting with the ten-cent call from a phone booth, provided high-stake gamblers are willing to risk playing a dime.

It's probably only right, the English phone service being what it is, that the cost is mercifully cheap. On our private phone one pence, or 2½ ¢ U.S., allows us local conversations lasting three minutes by day or a full twelve minutes after 6 P.M. and over the weekends. Toll calls are equally reasonable, which is just as well, because our conversations are hardly confined to the U.K. One evening I rang Zurich for 63 pence, or $1.57 U.S., plus tax, of course.

In England the phone bills are mailed out quarterly instead of monthly. Despite the fact that our phone amounts to a lifeline to civilization out in Oxford, London, and abroad, quarterly bills run little more than the regular monthly wallop back in New York City. For purposes of illustration, our last three *monthly* American statements ran $37.82, $41.20, and $38.16, while the first three *quarterly* English bills came to the equivalent of $47.20, $50.18, and $48.40.

In view of discount rates like that it's surprising that home phones still amount to a luxury item through the hill country we inhabit. With only nine million private phones in a land of more than fifty million people, national figures are modest enough. In Lower Slaughter, just one of the six cottages along the stream on either side of us is fitted with what Americans consider standard equipment.

"It's no trouble not being on the phone," one of the neighbors explained to me. "I make *me* few calls every week in the coin box up the track. It's no bother."

Although the chronic mechanical problems in England and America are much the same, several features of the native service are great improvements over what we'd been accustomed to. This applies especially to Information, or, in English, Enquiries. Many of the retarded girls I spoke with at 411 in Manhattan challenged me to repeat and sometimes even spell out the names of flourishing and well-known enterprises whose numbers I sought, such as Saks Fifth Avenue, the Waldorf-Astoria, and Sardi's.

But New York Telephone isn't alone in running a Just One Break personnel program. Of all the countless tribulations my father endured in his attempts to establish a voice link outside of Kane County, Illinois, the most memorable was the New Year's Eve when he tried to reach me on a person-to-person basis at a dinner party in New York. On the basis of long experience he slowly and distinctly told the operator he wanted to call R-o-b-e-r-t D-e-i-n-d-o-r-f-e-r at the number he just as carefully recited.

Of course Deindorfer isn't an easy name to spell—or to pronounce, either, for that matter—but the operator was having an especially hard time of it.

"No, no, Deindorfer doesn't start with a bee," he explained, his voice rising some. "It's dee, dee, dee like in Denver."

"Oh, it's Denver, Colorado, you want," Long Distance blankly replied.

My father leaned hard on a profanity, slammed the phone down, and retired without wishing me a happy 1959.

In England the operators have a basic grasp of spelling, not to mention good manners, which makes for a pleasant relationship even if the sound goes blotchy after they complete the call. A place name like Kidderminster needn't be broken down into component syllables for Enquiries to come up with the required inflated number. Better yet, she—or, more likely, he, the bulk of employees I tune in being male, for whatever that's worth—treats me with unfailing courtesy and cheer.

Along with audible good manners, telephone management in Old Blighty considers time, temperature, and Help Police as basic special service numbers for subscribers. The temperature is read in degrees Centigrade, sad to say, which takes a lot of doing for my wife, among others, who isn't good at figures, but the time of day comes through in a language we all of us understand, right down to the split-second.

The panoramic round-the-clock telephone information services include a canned pop tune called Dial-a-Disc, which is what more than forty million callers do every year despite the abundance of electric guitars on television and radio. For housewives interested in quite another concern, recipes are available every day. If the dishes run more to bland stews and shepherd's pies than five-star cuisine, well, at least they're practical, nutritious and inexpensive.

Technicians are understandably proud of the Father Christmas success they concocted several years ago. A series of recorded pauses—"Ho, Ho, Ho, and who's this phoning," followed by a gap long enough for the caller to offer up his name—gull millions of youngsters into believing they're having a give-and-take conversation with the British equivalent of Santa Claus.

Scotland runs daily ski reports during the season; Wales records its bedtime stories for children in what some Englishmen whimsically spell the Wellsh llanguage; London offers a canned special on what's doing for the young tourist, such as that 91-foot, 120-ton stuffed whale in the Natural History Museum.

In view of full-blown hit services on poetry, gardening, cricket matches, motoring reports detailed to specific detours, repairs, and traffic jams, and London tours in English, French, German, Spanish and Italian, it isn't surprising that the phone services can be addictive. Allen Jeffries, a London importer I know, won't

137

argue the point. On a business trip to the Continent one recent summer he couldn't resist casting a line from Munich, from Zurich, from Geneva, and, finally, from Rome simply to learn how the English cricket team was faring—badly, as usual—in its big test match with the West Indies.

My prosaic mass-produced taste doesn't run much to cricket, either dialing for scores or actually sitting in on the stuff, but I do have a favorite number of my own. Any time I want to draw a bead on ICI shares I ring up the daily stock prices and business news summary and prepare for the worst, such as off another two and a half points. ICI should do as well as that touring West Indian cricket team.

The canned information programs, the bargain price schedules, and the novelty of tuning in operators whose vocabulary includes good manners forbidden by Ma Bell can't help but please an itinerant American. They don't quite manage to offset the basic flaws in the service, mind you, but together they whittle down the level of my outrage. The system being what it is, that chronic ringing in my ears is more mechanical than psychological.

Whatever its mechanical defects, however, England's nationalized telephones have filled in a vagrant old aspiration. As the owner and proprietor of 3045120958, I have far more digits—if less amorous conversations—than the dudes who used to ring what looked like too many numbers on the silver screen at the Tivoli in Aurora.

Chapter 13

During a visit with a fishing friend in Wales several months after our own spawning run began I was well into a lyric monologue extolling the many pleasures of living in the United Kingdom, up to and specifically including the nine-pound roast chicken we'd just consumed right down to the wishbone, when our host interrupted to ask whether I had a few accompanying grumps.

"Oh yes," I said. "For one thing, my glass seems to be empty."

After the oversight was corrected I treated him to perhaps an hour of acerbic criticism of England, the English, and assorted English institutions. My reservations, although relatively few in number, are each of them sizzling.

For the sake of the record it's only fair to acknowledge several warps—defects is far too strong a word—of my own. A cup of tea isn't quite my cup of tea, native four-cylinder cars aren't my idea of comfortable transport whatever the astonishing mileage per gallon, and the adders lodging in the soft green countryside around us frighten me to death.

Along with that thin undercoating of bias I'm also subject to change with little or no notice. Every so often, especially if I'm running on less than a full tank of sleep, always a threat with a live cuckoo bird tuning up as early as 5:30 in the morning, the very English fixtures I normally find endearing can put me in a flaming rage. Such bittersweet reactions vary considerably. It's perfectly true, for example, that lowing herds do wind slowly o'er the lea, a host of daffodils is always to be seen in season, the lark at break of day doth arise. But it's also true that I nearly missed the train one morning when a lowing herd wound slowly o'er a stretch of single-track roadway I was driving in a hell-bent race to catch the 7:45 for London.

Normally, on a good day, I also don't mind correcting Joan's memory lapses on my way home from a productive afternoon at the Coach and Horses. A stop at the fishmonger, the butcher, the bakery, the ironmonger, the dairy, or the greengrocer can be a pleasant diversion, sociable, leisurely, touching a couple of fundamental chords. But receiving rush assignments based on lists the length of the sheets of subversives that Senator Joe McCarthy used to patriotically wave is quite another matter. In those bleak circumstances I've been known to wrathfully cry out for the jiffy one-stop shopping I've been accustomed to ever since I short-changed my mother after skinning through the back alley for a sack of provisions at Oxie's in Aurora.

In our rustic corner we've learned to make do without modern frills like buttered popcorn, instant cleaning and pressing, and round-the-clock pharmacies dispensing wonder cures for my round-the-clock afflictions. If I don't exactly relish polishing my own muddy boots, I do relish saving 75¢ a bandit named Ray charged for a curb-service shine on Third Avenue in New York City. On the slight chance that franchise fast-food chains qualify as essential conveniences, let it be recorded that England has joined the parade too; it now has the Little Chef Grill, one hundred of them at last count, and growing like a peptic ulcer, including one dangerously close to us, which we avoid the same way we avoided the gastronomic deadfalls that litter the American landscape.

Among the constant irks, nothing is more infuriating than the fact that the few commercial enterprises in nearby villages all shut tight as a drum between one and two every day, nothing, that is, except for the even more brazen fact that villages also close down for a full half day every week, Northleach on Tuesday, Stow-on-the-Wold Wednesday afternoon, Burford on Thursday.

Even when shops happen to be open, however, they're often not nearly as helpful as I'd like. All too frequently the specific items we seek—Swiss roll, canned applesauce, razor blades, toilet paper—are what they call temporarily out of stock, which means they might possibly be back on the shelves again sometime before Guy Fawkes Day. In case the goods are in stock, there's apt to be some transatlantic misunderstanding.

As a memorable case in point I recall the day I drove straight to my office to connect a new student-type desk lamp. But the plug on the end of the lamp was a size too small for the outlet, or power point, in the wall. On a piece of paper I drew the exact size of the light plug and the wall plug and set out for the ironmonger where I asked for a converter.

"That size is being phased out, sir," said a clerk whose nose didn't fit him very well, pointing to the sketch of the lamp plug.

"How long has this phasing out been underway?" I asked.

"It's hard to say, sir."

"Approximately, I mean. Five years? Ten? A century?"

The clerk suggested I bring the lamp in for a new plug. Did he know the size socket it was to fit? He gazed at my drawing, reached into a bin, and placed a replica socket on the counter.

Next morning, giddy to think I'd soon be able to actually see the typewriter keys I'd been drumming blindly, I stopped by the ironmongery with the prize lamp. A few turns of the screwdriver, a modest charge of 20 pence, or 50¢ U.S., an earful of the usual gratitude—everything was lovely until I got to the office and tried to light up. And so I learned that England has not two but three different socket sizes, three with the round points, that is, not to mention two more with square points. And so, after another long interlude playing the typewriter like a ground mole, I also learned the name Oliver & Newman Electrical Contractors, Ltd., one of whose chappies came round and made the necessary corrections there in the office.

As for that excessive gratitude on the part of the clerk, if there's one defect in the British character that sets my nerve ends to twanging, it's the sticky good manners everyone seems to have been born with, like bad teeth and a taste for sausage rolls. Not even stress situations dent the unfailing courtesy expected of adults and youngsters alike, including our own son, whose frequent lapses we charitably write off as rugged individualism.

At the start of our tour, when life was shiny new and refreshing, the formidable level of manners struck me as another dramatic improvement over what we had abandoned. I used to experience all too little of the stuff in the normal course of a day in New York City. But England echoed with a chorus of "cheerybye," "my apologies," and "thank you," emphatic stress on the word "you." From the moment the letter carrier slips our mail through the kitchen door with a hearty and bewildering "thank you" until the BBC4 radio announcer implores us to "have a pleasant sleep," the ritual amounts to a barrage of good cheer.

But before long I couldn't help but wonder whether the English aren't courteous to a fault. One raw windy day in the dead of winter I went so far as to breach the code by snapping back at a bearded chimney sweep hitting the usual conversational notes. "Thank you, sir," he said at the end of my tantrum.

Working stiffs as far down the prevailing social order as that chimney sweep and the dustmen who come by to collect trash on Wednesday forever fill out their assignments with the same cheery lip. Why does the poor waitress grown humpbacked carrying loads of starch from a kitchen reeking with bacon scents plump down our order with a kindly "thank you," as if she happens to be doing us a favor? Why does the ironmonger who personally insists on carrying fifty pounds of kitchen shelving out to the car defy the most elementary logic by offering up, once he catches his breath again, a ceremonial "thank you very much, sir"?

By the end of our first year I was willing to exchange the rhetorical courtesy for the grating rudeness of New York City. I longed to tune in on friends like Ray Robinson, witty and prickly, a magazine editor who regards himself as the world's foremost authority on tennis, baseball, civil rights, pizza pie, local, national and global politics, literature, paleontology, and other matters. Any time an inferior, which is to say someone else, so much as raises an idle question during one of Robinson's opinionated blast-offs, his voice starts to bristle with barbed wire. The prospect of him ever casting a line in English—"yes, Willie Mays might possibly be the finest ballplayer of his time, don't you think?"—fills me with hysteria.

Exceptions to the genteel British rule are so rare as to take root in the memory, like a great battlewagon of an Englishwoman, mostly wattles and suet, who came steaming up our walkway one summer, accompanied by a wrinkled little man, presumably her husband, and presumably not a mute, either, although she filled the air with such a blather that he never actually had the chance to offer up any proof of it.

"I expect you're the American who owns this," she said tersely.

I admitted as much.

"We've had our eye on your cottage for a long time, you know. You ought to sell to us."

"The cottage is not for sale. We're quite happy here."

My response would have discouraged most random inquiries. Our caller considered briefly—and tied on a different fly.

"The English don't care much for Yanks, you know. You'll never really get on with the people in the village."

Feeling the wind of that some, I was obliged to paint a picture of such transatlantic bliss that it must have sounded—at least I

143

implied as much—that Sir Anthony and Lady Milward across the stream were merely the most ornamental of the many local friends who queued up at the front gate imploring us to join them for lunch, dinner, cocktails, tennis, fishing, and even riding to hounds. The report was a bit extravagant. Although a number of neighbors had gone out of their way with demonstrations of kindness, such as a head of fresh lettuce, it was three months before we so much as met the Milwards and almost a year before we mutually did what passes for tea in England.

Still, the barnacled old lady seeking to wheedle us out of house and home seemed properly skewered. Even her husband blinked some, although I noticed he didn't break his silence. It was plainly no time to ease up.

"Besides, it's clear that you wouldn't fit in here." I paused for dramatic effect. "In Lower Slaughter there's a great stress on good manners."

Game, set, and match concluded, I spun round and strutted back into the cottage, triumphant, properly avenged, in full control. Or I was in full control until I gave my head another wallop on the stunted doorframe, anyway, which may have diminished the effect some.

Along with cloying good manners the general rule, friends and neighbors are unable to give a straightforward answer to basic two-plus-two type questions. They hedge, qualify, back off. After fishing regularly for more than a year one man still leans on the same props he employed the first night we didn't kill any trout together. One day, when I saw him using a pocket scale to weigh a big brown trout he bamboozled on a made-in-America streamer fly I'd loaned him, I put the usual question.

"Does that cock fish go over four pounds?"

"Oh, I wouldn't think he runs that much, would you?" he replied with the normal flourish, although later I managed to learn that the trout scaled exactly three-and-a-half pounds.

None of this ought to imply that English manners involve more form than substance. They don't. Genuine acts of kindness are so basic that a stranger from a far-off land comes to take them for granted after the initial shock wears off. Strangers step aside and smilingly open doors; Players who can't spell the Marquis of Queensbury remove their caps in coeducational lifts; people drive out of their way despite the stiff petrol prices to make certain visitors are following the directions they give.

Motorists elsewhere are normally even more insolent than pedestrians, but the English issue is especially well-behaved. Seated behind the wheels of their Vauxhalls and Hillmans, Rovers and Triumphs, these affable drivers are almost spastic as they cheerfully wave trailing cars around or acknowledge their thanks when an approaching vehicle squeezes to the edge of a narrow roadway in the interests of both principals' abiding good health.

But English English can also be far too formal in an increasingly casual era. Several men I know fairly well remain Mister to me, as I do to them, and I'm confused as to which party is supposed to finally break down the barrier. It was two years after I first met a near neighbor before he bashfully shuffled his feet some and suggested I call him Cyril.

At its higher levels the Mister Game is apt to take on some mysterious shadings. In our village one man is reported to fraternize not at all with another who made the mistake of addressing him by his Christian name before sufficient time had lapsed. The fact that the offended party is a full-blown patrician while the transgressor definitely isn't may have something to do with the breach, but I can't be sure.

Whether an outsider views all this as courtesy or affectation, these values are as familiar as the sound of the English voice, which needs no further amplification here. Despite a variety of regional flavors—some of the older rural Cotswold stock still pronounce the "s" like the "z," for instance—the tone of the language reminds me of what a departed friend named Bob Gurvitz used to say in a slightly different context. "Any time I want to have my sinus passages drained I just phone up Boston," he'd remark.

What makes the stiff sounds more difficult still is the fact that English English can be every bit as foreign as Veps or Khond. Just when I suspect I'm finally tuning in on things—first floor for second floor, right, knickers for milady's undies, layabout for bum—some new brick of language knocks me for a loop. One night I was successfully unwinding the usual daily inventory of calamities on BBC1's evening news when the announcer got around to an international golf match. "Going into tomorrow's play," he said, so help me, "England is level-pegging it with the United States." He finished with a typical rhetorical audience participation: "So the match suddenly looks difficult for England, doesn't it?"

As an Air Force friend based in the United Kingdom explained during a sociable briefing while I was still suffering from culture shock, the language gap isn't restricted entirely to oral conversations. Any American old enough to retire his bib is familiar with the mute abusive one-finger fork. In England the vulgar cipher involves not one but two fingers, spread out in the shape of a V, same as President Nixon used to flash adoring crowds during moments of plastic jubilation. In view of his obvious contempt for citizens whose tax contributions underwrote some $17 million worth of improvements on his various private homes, I can't help but think—at the risk of my psychiatric file being rustled some dark night, for reasons of national security—that maybe our former jim-dandy old prexy is manually fluent in another language.

As a general rule, however, the English aren't especially addicted to profanity in either a vocal or digital form. Not even a four-alarm accident changes their tune. In the strictly masculine preserve of a nearby garage I once saw a mechanic drop an iron carjack on his foot, drop to the oily floor, and painfully moan without ever permitting himself the luxury of some healing catch-all profanity.

Given such standards, my own frequent falls from grace have been known to startle the residents. Playing some tennis at a club

146

that enrolled me before anyone realized that my speech habits, like my backhand, aren't all they ought to be, I let a crucial shot sizzle past me at the net. My reaction—"Godalmighty," nothing more—was downright meek under the circumstances. Yet the shock and alarm registered even before my partner judiciously pulled me aside: "I say, you might mind your language with ladies present."

Among other things, I resent Sunday newspapers that run to only thirty or forty pages, warm beer without much of a kick to it, and rambling old firetrap hotels not fitted with proper escape ladders. Hallways lined with turn-of-the-century red fire buckets filled to the brim don't exactly assuage my fears, either.

If anything, the native handwriting screws my frustrations tighter still. As one of the few living Americans who consistently failed to win even the basic Palmer Method badge at Mary A. Todd School in Aurora, an underprivileged welt in the crucial formative years that might account for all my ensuing instabilities, I'd feel a certain sympathy for other blotchy penmen if they didn't fall so far short of my own shameful mark. What makes it all the worse is the fact that illegible signatures frequently call for a direct reply. My gorge still rises as I recall the morning the post included a letter from the Hardy Brothers fishing tackle people in London, who were mending a broken rod tip of mine, beautifully typed right down to the bottom where the customary chicken tracks appeared. I had a chance of addressing my reply simply to Hardy Brothers or to what the signature appeared to read, B. X. Blmed, although I didn't think many Armenians were doing business in Pall Mall. Finally I sent it out To Whom It May Concern at Hardy's. Back came a legible response up to the theatrical finish, an equally abstruse but slightly different—perhaps a cousin?—Armenian-looking name.

Anyone who suspects I exaggerate the bleak state of British letters is invited to consider a jiffy market research test I conducted one week. Even my wife, whose vision, being several years less worn than mine, is also several points higher, managed to decipher merely two of eleven incoming letters, one of them, from Michael Hall, an easy lay-up shot.

Despite the many pleasures of living in England, I've also learned to loathe pork pies, lighter fluid that doesn't last me through a deck of cigarettes, and the long geologic wait for shoe repairs, tailoring, and the plumber, but I expect it could be worse. Bobby Waters, a schoolmaster in Cornwell, still hadn't got his Woolseley 15–60 back five years after he dropped it off at a local garage for rust treatment and a respray. "Frankly, I think Mr. Waters can't have been in his right mind leaving it with me for so long," the repairman commented in hopes of reassuring any future customers. "If I had been him I'd have moved it to another garage after three months."

But no roll call of my reservations regarding the English is complete without some reference to the goosey fairy tale feelings Gentlemen and Players alike have for the Royal Family. Soon after we alighted I experienced a demonstration of these sentiments when an American magazine assigned me an article exposing the size of the private fortune as opposed to the Buckingham Palace and Crown Jewels type hereditary fortune of Her Majesty Elizabeth II, by the Grace of God, of the United Kingdom of Great Britain and Northern Ireland and of Her Other Realms and Territories, Queen, Head of the Commonwealth, Defender of the Faith, and so on. This meant I had to slip into my trench coat and play ace reporter there for a couple of weeks.

On asking a horsy neighbor in Slaughter if he could put me onto someone able to accurately estimate the bottom-line value of all the Queen's horses, which came to a total of twenty-two thoroughbreds at the time, he positively sputtered. Once he got a grip on himself again he explained that the reigning sovereign —yes, folks, that's what he said—was entitled to some privacy, pronounced priv-, not prive-, ah-see, especially in the matter of the personal fortune, which my subsequent research fixed at $40 million. Obviously I'd committed a breach of lese majesty so vile that, unless I conducted myself with more discretion, a week entwined in the stock on the village green in nearby Stow-on-the-Wold might be the least of my comeuppance.

For what it's worth, I have no quarrel with the Queen, a decent, pleasant, upright ornament who performs functions like banging a few subjects across the shoulder blades and pronouncing them knights with a practiced skill. Young Prince Charles seems all right too, engaging and sincere, well-motivated, a can't-miss prospect who should become a whizbang king when he gets his turn at bat.

Since presumably only God has a say in the matter, my own opinions here don't have any real bite to them, but I could do without the rest of the family—I don't have the foggiest how they feel about me—with an emphasis on Princess Anne, a peevish, mean-spirited girl whose Royal Wedding nearly drove me to anarchy. The pageantry, the romantic haze, the synthetic cotton candy the last few days before the main event reached a crescendo so hysterical that a local woman whose taste, judgment, and vision generally are what the British call spot on was actually heard to say, "Lovely, Princess Anne looked lovely on the telly last evening, didn't she?"

The question wasn't quite the rhetorical flourish she thought it to be. Despite all the Royal Beauticians, the princess didn't, doesn't and won't ever look lovely, a great pity, I suppose, although her husband, a toy soldier with a pennywhistle brain, has good looks enough to cover the both of them. The American actress Candy Bergen—the word lovely positively applies in her case—hit it about right the night a television commentator asked her impressions of Princess Anne, whom she had met in Africa.

"Well, the word 'constipated' always comes to mind," Miss Bergen thoughtfully replied.

For all my New World detachment on the matter, however, I was as outraged and sickened as any resident Colonel Blimp—several perfect replica models of whom I've encountered, by the way—when that stray crazy shot up the limousine in which the newlyweds were riding. In a world ominously out of joint, security should definitely be tightened considerably. But I must confess to a lingering incidental reaction: in case anyone in the Royal Family ever does get bushwhacked, God forbid, better Anne than mums or Charlie.

Chapter 14

Since we uncovered what amounts to a made-to-measure shopping service soon after settling in England, the Deindorfers in
general and the principal shareowner in particular have managed
to accumulate a few treasures we never seriously expected to call
our own. Such miracles happen, not often, but often enough to
melt our limited assets down.

Our first success involved nothing more than a fishing reel, a
3⅜-inch Perfect fly reel by Hardy Brothers of London, to be
exact, in my own view the finest reel ever built, so superior to
other competitive models that management stopped making
them, like the Packard automobile. My search for an out-of-print
Perfect commenced long before we left New York. In the beginning I employed the conventional ways and means, which is to
say I contacted some of the better tackle shops, Abercrombie &
Fitch, Orvis, Mills, The Anglers' Roost, on the off chance they
might have a good clean Perfect hidden away among their used
stock. Sadly, sadly, they didn't.

Meanwhile, I kept beating the water with another Hardy product, a nice reel, too, only not quite the heavier eye-fed model so much a part of my aspirations. Any time I made a bad cast, which was all too often, I told myself that somehow it wouldn't have happened if I'd been fishing a Perfect.

For obvious reasons my pulse accelerated some when we finally packed off to England. One of our first stops during the decompression stopover in London was the Hardy retail outlet, where I made the usual inquiries in hopes of a little hands-across-the-sea understanding.

"We have quite a large waiting list—twenty or twenty-five names—in case a Perfect in the size you require comes in, which is seldom," a man in the used tackle section below stairs said flatly. "Of course if you want to leave your name and address. . . ."

At that point the wind went out of my illusions. I continued going through the motions by running an ad in the English publication *Trout and Salmon*, skinning into tackle shops in Oxford and Stratford, Banbury and Cheltenham, asking British anglers if they had any leads. But down in my waistband where reality lurks I got the feeling my quest was futile.

All of a sudden, however, I found myself talking with a vigorous leathery bloke, Bill Hudson, whose gap-toothed face I'd spotted in a London newspaper. Town criers are alive and well and living in tradition-laden England. If Bill Hudson of Shipston-on-Stour, twelve miles away, isn't the best of the lot, at least he did finish third in the town crier competition at Hastings, which is why his picture had appeared in the paper.

For a price of 80 pence, or $2 U.S., Hudson agreed to put on his official tricorner green hat with gold braid, red jacket, green breeches, yellow shoes, and buckled shoes, and, resplendent as a peacock, offer up a commercial word on my behalf the following night, as it happened.

Hear him:

"Oyez, oyez, oyez! American willing pay twelve pounds for

Hardy Brothers Perfect Model trout reel, size three and three-eighths, in good condition. God Save the Queen!"

Ringing his seventeenth-century brass bell, his voice practically lifting off neighboring slate rooftops, Hudson moved on to the next street, and the next, and the next. Altogether he cried out my message a total of forty times.

In a matter of days I was the proud owner of a fine old Hardy Perfect, at my price of twelve pounds, or $30 U.S., plus the original stake for hiring out Hudson's celebrated lungs, which was a marvelous experience, except for one thing. We promptly developed a habit we haven't yet been able to kick.

Once we tuned in on Bill Hudson's prowess, Joan and I realized we had hit upon the means to other ends—a Knole settee, a triangular oak washstand, antique oak joint stools, an Austin Princess Vandenplas 4 litre R motorcar, the R significant because it stands for a Rolls-Royce engine, an old thumbscrew, and also a second Perfect reel. With a shopping list as abundant as that, it dawned on me that Hudson, while wonderfully gifted, wasn't the only town crier still operating in the United Kingdom.

At last count the total consisted of approximately forty other men whose diminishing profession stretches back to the thirteenth century, situated in towns like Wells, Bodman, Marlborough, and Guildford, including Herbert ("Whisper") Waldron in Great Barringtown, a renowned and colorful crier said to have such a shattering muzzle velocity that local farmers book him to scare the crows away after fields are freshly planted. Over the centuries these grass-roots communicators have enlarged their original "Twelve o'clock and all is well" charter to include not only election returns, garden fetes, and other civic events but also commercial messages such as lost spectacles and my fishing reel.

We didn't take on the full network, which might have rolled into too much money, but we did hire out a geographic sampling —Hudson, Bumper Howells in Hay-on-Wye just across the line in Wales, E.H. Preston in Tewkesbury, twice national champion.

Preston turned out to be especially helpful. At one point he even gave me a discount hitchhike: "If you are stuck for a Christmas present for your husband or son, visit Avonlec Fishing Tackle Shop on Barton Street, Tewkesbury. Also sort your old tackle out and look for a Hardy Perfect three and three-eighths trout reel for which we will pay a good price." Informal price scales varied, with Howell's fee of 50 pence, or $1.25 U.S., and a pint of beer, the lowest we have encountered.

For all their deafening enterprise, the town criers we employ from time to time don't always give us bottom-line results. Even the least expensive Knole settee they turned out was too rich for our budget, and we looked at three washstands without seeing one we liked. But we did add a joint stool; I found a second Hardy Perfect; and that glistening four-door dream standing in the village square is positively a Princess 4 Litre R.

Our transactions with assorted town criers haven't been confined to fanning Britain for antique cars and antique fishing tackle. On the basis of a little discreet planning, we treated two visiting American relatives to a surprise earful the weekend they came out to see how the family exiles were getting on. During what they assumed was a casual trip through the surrounding landscape I drove into High Street in Shipston bang on schedule at 6 P.M. Materializing from behind the war memorial in his cocked hat and white cravat, Hudson lifted a seven-pound brass bell and let go:

"Shipston-on-Stour extends a hearty welcome to visiting American guests Grace Greene Brown and Helen Greene Ross. God Save the Queen!"

After Hudson shook hands and stepped into a nearby pub, presumably to invest a share of that 80 pence I'd furtively handed over, I switched off a recorder hidden in the front seat of the car and gave the relatives a cassette to carry home as Exhibit A in case anyone in the bridge club doubted the fact that they'd been officially anointed during their travels through Old Blighty.

Quite apart from their obvious utilitarian contributions—and just recently I added a seventeenth-century crossbow to the shopping list—those ornamental town criers illustrate a traditional age-haunted aspect of British life almost overwhelming for a Midwestern American. During the sizzling Great Depression, when I was a boy, my hometown went to elaborate lengths to organize a festive centennial celebration. For months adult males grew beards, housewives turned from darning old socks to stitching up period costumes, schoolchildren composed subject-verb-predicate essays and rehearsed for the big parade. The event was all we'd hoped it might be. Through a dim tunnel of years I can picture it still—fireworks, lemonade, pie-eating contests, three-legged races and other competitions, bearded residents in costumes, Civil War veteran Dan Wedge trundled past in a parade sweeping from the Burlington Railway along Broadway to the firehouse—the wistful memories of a quieter, simpler time.

Subsequently, my parents packed us into the family Reo Flying Cloud, a picnic cooler strapped to one running board, and we drove to Naperville, St. Charles, and, if I'm not mistaken, also Sugar Grove to see those neighboring communities go through the same emotional binge. Back in the nineteen thirties reaching the age of one hundred was a popular sport for small towns in Illinois, like making root beer and watching donkey baseball.

In view of my reflex reaction that a centennial was something to be celebrated with fireworks and parades, it wasn't surprising that I suffered mild culture shock once we alighted in such a ripe old land. From the moment we embarked on the usual trips to Stonehenge and Bath, where I drank gagging sulphur-flavored water washing through pipes the Romans laid nearly two thousand years ago, I found myself caught up in antiquity. On balance, it's an exhilarating sensation.

Better still, artifacts are to be found everywhere here in the Cotswolds. Less than a mile from our cottage we drive onto the Fosseway, for instance, straight as a string, two lanes unwinding for more than a hundred miles, a line of roadway originally laid in the second century. Among other encounters with old age,

155

we've stopped at a thirteenth-century inn, walked into a barn built five hundred years ago, had a one-star dinner at a three-star restaurant time-stamped the fourteenth century. On a visit to Devon a retired farmer who, while he wore his long years lightly, seemed a bit of an antique himself, insisted on walking me to a cottage built in the tenth century. "He ought to know," a friend remarked later. On the trip to Hastings for the town criers' competition we stopped at a venerable hotel whose oak-paneled lobby is adorned with a dandy Stephen Potter inscription: "*Rebuilt* in 1420."

In antique shops crowding the High Street in neighboring villages Joan and I have looked at pewter, silver, oak, and walnut so old the vendor who writes the floater policy on our household effects back in New York City would instantly double the annual premium if we ever were to crate any home with us, if and when, I might add, if and when. Despite fairly steep prices—the cost of antiques is an exception to the relatively cheap regional economic rule—we have bought some antiques, among them several lovely poacher's canes, which open up into guns or fishing rods instead of swords, without using a town crier as interlocutor.

But personally, one of the most impressive old pieces I've yet to see is a gleaming 1916 Model T Ford in mint condition, with spoked wooden wheels, brass radiator and sidelamps, a ghost of my boyhood, fitted with a right-hand drive that suggests Old Henry wasn't above squeezing the sterling market despite his well known Anglophobia. To my surprise, the Tin Lizzie didn't even draw a crowd the morning a collector wearing a white motoring cap drove it slowly through Bourton.

Generally, the English are blasé about back numbers so dated that bold and enterprising Americans might be selling tickets to see them after the Tastee Freeze concession is finished. The day we went past a bakery in business for over seven hundred years in Chipping Camden I expressed an interest in an intriguing shape standing in the garden behind an old home in Bourton.

"Oh, that. It's a dovecote, not as big as the one at the Manor House, but quite a nice dovecote all the same. It's in the Domesday Book."

On the off chance my source was being extravagant, next time I visited the library I checked to see whether the stone and timber structure actually was listed in the official inventory of castles, houses, and other properties compiled for William the Conquerer shortly after his landing in 1066. Sure enough. Given my Midwestern concept of age I couldn't resist the urge to climb a moldering staircase up into the top of the dovecote.

If that experience amounted to powerful stuff for me, Joan, who grew up in a relatively old section of America, North Carolina, can't blot out the memory of her talk with an amateur local historian. During a windy talk devoted to landmark structures in the general area, such as a relic barn Shakespeare was said to have slept in back in his poaching phase, the historian cited our own digs for the sake of contrast.

"A cottage like this is fairly new, two hundred and fifty, perhaps three hundred years old, which isn't much at all, is it?" he said.

Yet nothing illustrates the casual English approach to antiquity more emphatically than a brief lapse the day a crew of four mechanics was trying to mend what remained of the brakes on our secondhand car, circa 1969. In the midst of a critical consultation up on the rack, one mechanic hopped off, spoke with an angular lady who had toddled into the garage, stuffed an envelope she gave him in a back pocket, and rejoined his playmates.

"She had one of the blokes in Oxford date a coin I picked up in *me* garden fortnight ago," he explained.

"Well, did he date it?"

"She said he did." He opened the envelope. "Yes, it's dated three hundred seventy four dash three eighty A.D."

It was a small coin, dark, the edges scalloped, a woman's profile stamped on both sides, with good definition to it. Feeling almost foolish to be holding money minted sixteen hundred years earlier, I asked what he planned to do with the coin.

"I haven't thought about it, really. Put it in a tin with the others I've found, I expect," he said.

For all its tingling excitement, however, antiquity isn't altogether a blessing, at least not for me, largely because I happen to measure six feet, three-and-a-half inches, or rather more than bygone Englishmen, among them the chaps who built our cottage. Consequently, life amounts to an abiding obstacle course— and, as the dents on my skull painfully illustrate, it's a course I haven't mastered. Although some of our ceilings measure a full six feet six, the front porch, the front doorway, the step into the kitchen, and the approach to the bedroom measure less than I do, which is why we have a family laugh, or 50 percent of the resident adults have a family laugh, every time I give my head what the British call a jolly good crump.

Out beyond our malevolent doorway, out in stunted villages huddled in the Cotswold hills, less familiar, equally painful, more forbidding perils await me. I recall a one-bump comfort stop at a public convenience in Moreton-in-Marsh, a two-bump visit— this one actually drew blood—at the Windrush Book Shop in Burford, and a three-bump dinner at the Old Mill in Withington. As of this writing my most serious injury came when I was bushwhacked in a Hampshire village named, so help me, Nether Wallop, to a point where some of that come-and-get-it national medical treatment was required.

"You better wear a crash helmet around the house," Joan suggested after an especially hellish collision.

"They don't make crash helmets big enough for Daddy's head," Scott said with the normal show of respect.

At the suggestion of a town crier we hired our first summer, I visited a Stratford arms and armor shop bristling with pikestaffs and halberds, dueling pistols and old muskets. But what interested me the most was a suit of chain mail visibly a perfect fit on a wooden dummy whose dimensions came to only five feet, three inches. Apparently I registered an edge of surprise.

"That was the typical height back in olden times, you know," the proprietor assured me.

Of course it was. And of course on my way out I banged my twentieth-century nob on an olden-times beam despite one of those recurring Mind Your Head signs they ought to wire with yellow warning lights.

Chapter 15

Up he came, once, twice, three times, pinwheeling, splashing water, fanning his thick tail, a fish the size of a daydream, an awesome brown trout sullenly trying to shake the number 16 fly hooked in the hinge of his massive jaw.

That particular trout wasn't the biggest fish in the river, not by a few pounds, but at least he was sufficient for a date with the nearest taxidermist, which was exactly what I had in mind. Surely the biggest brown trout I ever hooked on a dry fly ought to be nailed on the library wall back in New York City for skeptical friends who might suspect I was stretching things a little.

The rod point high, the line taut without straining the 4x leader, I played the fish slowly while my bearded English ghillie stood in his wading boots close by supplying a running pep talk. A ghillie does something more than take a visitor to his beat, recommend specific flies, point to where the trout are lying, net, and clean the fish. He also leads you straight to a pint of beer afterwards.

Except for the occasional sound of my prize trout hitting the water, the speckled afternoon was peaceful and still. Some ducks lazed below us, cows grazed on a rolling hillside, a willow tree fluttered in the wind near the river's edge. Along the far bank, in a garden behind a thatch-roofed stone cottage, a withered old man in a deerstalker hat stood silently watching us.

If fishing has its holy waters, they must be the Test and the Itchen, picture postal rivers, both of them, clear and cold, coiling through green meadowland in the hills of southern England. Men whose names are a part of fishing folklore—Skues and Halford, Lord Grey and Hewitt, Ritz and Wulff—have cast, cast, cast their greased lines on these classic Hampshire chalkstreams. Better still, Izaak Walton, the original, father of us all, the illustrious old boy himself, frequently wet a line on the Itchen the last few seasons of his life.

All at once my epic trout boiled down the river along some bullrushes. As I checked the line only a bit, he was gone, the leader snapped off, captive no longer, free to swim the River Test until someone more patient, more skillful, more accustomed than I to walloping big trout safely brought him to the net.

"You lost him!" An unmistakable edge of reproach tightened my ghillie's English accent. "You didn't give him line enough, did you, and you lost him."

Later that day, after replaying the wretched scene over again in my mind, it struck me that his brief analysis wasn't altogether accurate. Oh, I'd lost him all right, lost the trout due to careless fishing, but another Englishman had put the disaster into softer focus.

"Nay, the trout is not lost; for pray take notice, no man can lose what he never had."

Who wrote it? Who else?

In warming myself on familiar lines from that same standard

source, I realized it was time to settle an old account. Despite the astonishing fish I'd missed, I'd caught seven respectable trout that day, more than enough for neighboring skillets back in Lower Slaughter, along with countless other fish in other waters in other seasons. A vagabond American thankful for years of angling can hardly be blamed for paying proper respects when he gets the chance.

First thing next morning I drove to Winchester, nine miles away, located the magnificent Norman Cathedral, parts of which date back to the eleventh century, and walked through massive outer doors. There in the cathedral's south transept, in a small chapel with stained-glass windows, one of them a pastoral scene of the neighboring River Itchen I was to fish that day, the remains of Izaak Walton lie buried under a memorial stone.

Gazing at the text on the stone I realized that Walton offered impressive evidence that the old aphorism about the days a devotee spends fishing not counting against his allotted span might be more than a wistful hope. Back in an era when most people didn't live much longer than a fruitfly, The Compleat Angler not only stretched his life to a full ninety seasons but lasted until the winter of 1683 when game fishing shut down for the year.

But my visit to the River Test and Walton's shrine illustrates something every bit as important as actuarial tables. England is scaled to a wonderfully convenient size. Only 580 miles from top to bottom and 275 miles across its broadest width, the whole of the country is within reach of the four-cylinder wheels we spin every chance we have.

In the realm of angling, I've not confined my sport to the River Test of song and legend. I've also developed character not catching nearly as many fish as I'd like on the Exe and Taw in Devon, the Lugg in Hereford, the Rutterwater in Westmorland, the Wear in Durham, the Wye in Wales, and Loch Leven in Scotland. Hopefully, it won't be long before I work the Nith, the Tay, the Tweed, and several other celebrated waters I've been devotedly apprenticing for ever since I first fished doughballs for carp in the River Fox in northern Illinois.

But our family travels haven't been as self-serving as they might sound. Over the seasons we've also taken advantage of Great Britain's convenient dimensions to build sand castles on Brownsea Island and Bournemouth on the south coast, explore a limestone cave in Wycombe, tune in another language around Brecon in Wales, visit Bath, Ledbury, and Coventry—in the last, the inscription across the old bombed-out World War II altar, over which they've run up the modern cathedral, catches at the throat: "Father, Forgive Them"—and walked the promenade at Hastings.

"Let's go look at England washing into the sea at the end of Cornwall," Joan suggested one day.

"Okay. Let's."

Off we went, the boot of the car stacked with fresh fruit and soft drinks, through Cheltenham and Bristol, across Wiltshire and Somerset, riding comfortable motorways to Exeter, skinning west on smaller tracks through stunning country. The landscape slowly changed character as the hours unwound, clear out to Land's End something more than two hundred miles from our cottage.

While double- and even more hazardous single-track roads abound in rural areas, England boasts an impressive grid of what they call dual carriageways, two or three lanes of one-way traffic on either side of a planted center safety strip, much like American thruways except that the carriageways, being part of a moderately socialist state, have no toll booths, cost motorists nil, and are kept in a fine state of repair. It's probably just as well that the carriageways aren't littered with petrol stations every so many miles, because, if England is fairly small, the staff help I encounter any time I need assistance—I often depend on the kindness of strangers myself—is smaller still. Many of them don't have the foggiest awareness of guidebook sights only miles away.

Even now I go cold recalling to mind an experience with an attendant manning the pumps near Stow whose ignorance was as profuse as his acne. In my innocence I asked whether he could direct me toward Warwick Castle, an especially popular landmark relic attracting visitors from all points on the compass. He blinked, ran a forlorn hand through his haystack coiffure, and allowed he had no idea. Since it couldn't be far whatever the direction, I indulged a basic impulse by inquiring how long he'd lived in that area.

"All *me* life," he said proudly, the point of my query plainly eluding him.

Two miles straight up the road, a track he must have traveled many a day, an arrowed sign pointed the way: Warwick 26 miles.

Castles and palaces, cathedrals and Roman digs, are routine tourist fare throughout England, of course, but even more intriguing events are also scheduled on summer weekends within easy driving range. Hot-air balloon competitions, chariot races, outdoor symphonies, narrowboat trips up the canals, town crier championships, horse shows, Morris dancers, and gang jousts with men and their horses both dressed in medieval regalia crowd the calendar—and the village of Eyam in Derbyshire produces a dandy little plague commemoration each August.

Not every last one of those events turns out to be a winner, for geography isn't the only small-scale aspect of our corner of England. In the spring of our first full year, several children, our own among them, whom I hadn't suspected could read much more than candy wrappers, displayed an electrifying ability to decode the whole of the typically hyperbolic circus billboards displayed in shop windows, which explains why I found myself transporting a carload of young hysterics ten miles to Northleach on a sunny afternoon I'd rather have devoted to some diversion of my own. While I had gently cautioned the child who shares my name that this rustic big top wouldn't measure up to the vast brassy Ringling Brothers, Barnum and Bailey or the Moscow circus he'd eaten his way through back in Madison Square Garden, or even England's better circuses, for that matter, I was in no way prepared for anything quite so modest, although, to be perfectly fair about it, the ticket price of 20 pence, or 50¢ U.S., was a bit more modest than I'd been accustomed to too.

An ominous and, as things developed, blindingly accurate preview of what was to follow commenced with the very first act, extravagantly ballyhooed by the ringmaster as England's Most Spectacular Trained Horse, which turned out to be a scruffy little gray, its tail stiff with manure, and a young girl hobbling with one leg encased in Plaster of Paris from ankle to thigh, the act accompanied by a scratchy recording of what sounded—the record was so worn it was difficult to tell for certain—like Ravel's *Bolero*. At the first commanding crack of the whip England's Most Spectacular Trained Horse bolted over the ring barrier, tipped over a vending table, and ran out behind what passed as the big top. Two roustabouts—the romantic whiff of sawdust so overpowering to one of them that I spotted him in other incarnations later, first as a clown and then as a juggler, although he seemed most comfortable in the roustabout role—pushed the horse back into the ring, but he was plainly off his feed. The trainer soon gave it up as a bad job, dejectedly limping out of the ring to be replaced by what the ringmaster lyrically described as England's Most Comical Clowns, including the roustabout, which, if the description was accurate, well, God help England.

The remainder of the circus—the juggler, three female acrobats bolted from some home for the physically handicapped, a fire-eater, a ballet danced by a gap-toothed crone in a playsuit—was so inferior that I didn't know whether to laugh or cry. The diversion mercifully came to an end with a dog act, what else, two dogs and Princess Carolla, whom I'd first encountered at the ticket office and later when she sold me a few franks for my wards. She exited to thunderous applause, including a vigorous ration from my heir, which suggests something or other about formative tastes, I expect.

Despite an occasional bust like the circus, however, England offers so many assorted sights within easy distance that we've organized a regular excursion for weekend guests. We drive them to see an alien redwood tree rising over Wyck Rissington two miles away, to Tewkesbury for the town crier surprise, to Oxford and Stratford-on-Avon, to the Roman villa at Chedworth, and sometimes to Cheltenham for luxury shopping, all of those areas within thirty miles of us.

Without traveling too far, it's also possible to take a number of different specialty tours for visitors who have some personal warp—antique shop tours, fishing tours, castle and cathedral tours, even narrow-gauge rail tours for outright kinks. As a one-time English lit major whose rusty memory still registers scraps of the tipsy old music—For ever wilt thou love, and she be fair ... And that one talent which is death to hide ... I met a stranger from an antique land ... She loved me for the dangers I had passed ... Where Alph the sacred river ran through caverns measureless to man—I actually have seen that country church-yard, Dr. Johnson's house, Canterbury, the Lake Country, and the very room in which Shakespeare was born.

Although I hadn't realized it beforehand, an especially intoxicating experience awaited me as we slowly moved south through the Wye Valley one springtime. A thin sun warmed the skies; new lambs suckled their mothers in rolling green fields along the way. Without any warning we saw it standing off to our left, a weatherbeaten old ruin, a pile of old stone, Tintern Abbey, on a hillside, the River Wye tumbling far below, the scene so stunning it cried out for an artist. For a long moment that morning Wordsworth's pantheism looked a good bet.

Geography such as England's offers youngsters a different type of bonanza. Just nine miles away lies the fulfillment of even the most extravagant childhood dreams: snorkels, hook-and-ladder units, tenders, water wagons, the whole catalogue, the Fire Service Technical College at Moreton-in-Marsh, whose student body of some 3,000 consists of undergraduate smoke-eaters from more than fifty countries come to actually see how a variety of demonstration fires can be effectively doused. It's an easy drive to riverboat trips, caves, game preserves, the home base for the RAF's famous Red Arrow precision stunt fliers, and Mother Goose settings like Banbury and St. Ives.

Once Scott's interests ascended to the level of Robin Hood we did more than help him string his first bow. North of Nottingham, in what is now increasingly coal-mining country, we walked what's left of Sherwood Forest, squeezed inside the hollow Major Oak the Merry Men are said to have hidden in— "Daddy, how did Friar Tuck fit in here?"—and stopped at the antique church in Edwinstowe where, according to what locals insist is more than a legend, Robin Hood made an honest woman of Maid Marian.

On that trip to Nottingham and other trips before and since I've found that Deindorfer's First Motoring Law applies in England as much as it does in America. As a small-town child growing up during the Great Depression I constantly heard otherwise informed people, my dear father among them, insist that the best place to stop for a meal was where truck drivers gathered. I suppose it had a certain tinny logic to it, especially in the hardscrabble nineteen thirties, if only because truckers, whatever their wages nowadays, had as little money as the rest of us, maybe less, and their long miles on the road seemed to qualify them as authorities on exactly which diners stretched a dime, or perhaps even a quarter, the furthest.

At the same time, the formula ignored the basic fact that most truckers are jovial stalwarts with cast-iron digestive systems who judge a café more in terms of quantity than quality, not to mention such convivial contributions to the ambience as a jukebox or television and waitresses shaped like the gatefold in big circulation magazines some of these knights of the road have been known to glance through.

On the basis of two grievous lapses when the clock ran out without any food in sight except rest stops filled with great lorries, I know my own First Motoring Law is to be heeded in the

United Kingdom too: any time you see a café popular with transport types hit the accelerator hard and keep right on going.

For children, London amounts to the end of the rainbow. It's filled with the Changing of the Guard and other ceremonial rain dances, Kentucky Fried Chicken shops, the Tower of London, infinite films and plays, the Serpentine, and the National History Museum, in which the 92-foot, 120-ton blue whale is a particular delight. One eventful weekend we treated our son to a splendid English monument, the Globetrotters, the Harlem Globetrotters, at Wembley Stadium: Meadowlark Lemon, Marquis Haynes, the old familiar faces, to cloudburst applause, which indicates that superior slapstick tends to travel well.

Despite the marvelous opportunities that abound in easy range, however, it wasn't long before we realized that not every classmate in the village school has sopped up the sights in London. On hearing Scott give a play-by-play of the blue whale for a peer, I was struck dumb to hear him politely ask what a museum was. Horning in at that point myself, I patiently explained it was a great pile of a building stuffed with dinosaur bones, Egyptian mummies, and other artifacts like a gift and card shop.

With Paris, Zurich, Amsterdam, and the Scandinavian land mass only an hour or so away by air, we widened our horizons some during holidays, pleased that Daddy was flying again after several grounded years as a card-carrying member of the Newton-Was-Right Club, official slogan "The Best Airplane Ever Built Was The Santa Fe Chief." We watched windmills slowly spin in Holland, rode ferryboats to off-islands, went up the Jungfrau in Switzerland, almost high enough for a nosebleed—none of those travels theoretically aimed at showing an evolving manchild a bit of the world a bad idea for a sinner on the sunny side of fifty, either.

But the fact that so many wonders are in easy range of Lower Slaughter in no way implies that local happenings raised to the status of major events are to be belittled. They aren't. Youngsters who've seen Malta or France, Italy or Germany, haven't lost crucial perspective when it comes to something like a grand parade scheduled for Bourton toward the end of our first spring in residence. Traffic from all over the backlands converged on High Street a full hour before the parade was scheduled to unwind.

Even now I must admit to being impressed by the brassy sound rising in the April air as the parade finally pushed off. Bugles blaring, great tuba horns thumping, drums rattling, the march music a sprightly number, the Gloucestershire Regimental Band of some fifty men stepped by in their bright red coats, the familiar leopardskins draped over the shoulders of the percussionists, a drum major goosing along in a strutty step. After all our years a mere two blocks from Fifth Avenue, up which parades literally miles long sweep every few weeks, my eyes glazed over with the love-a-parade excitement, and I eagerly awaited the rest of it, which was my mistake. At the other end of town the band reversed direction and came back playing the same song, which may well have been the only one they knew. The parade that drew such a boisterous crowd consisted of the band—nothing more.

Personally, I got to wondering what the occasion for such civic fervor could be. But I ought to have known. Parked in the middle of town stood a trailer emblazoned with recruiting posters for the British Army. Several decorated troopers in full uniform were available to answer questions, trying to sign on a few new recruits to be sent through basic training and perhaps packed off to Ireland where they could be blown to bits if the supply of target women and children happened to be running short for the IRA provos.

But for us, the small scale of England remains a natural asset we put to good use. Whatever direction the sights we want to see lie, the bounty of the lovely land is invariably within range of a car and a blank weekend, even heartbreak Ireland, which seems to be spinning closer all the time.

Chapter 16

Until just recently, when the ominous tick of a calendar hanging over the slot machine in our kitchen here in Lower Slaughter became too insistent to ignore any longer, Joan and I had studiously avoided any serious discussion of the fact that our English adventure was coming to an end, in the hopes it might go away, like a toothache or a bad dream, which are very much the same thing.

But with the last few months of our tour beginning to melt away we've finally held a series of no-nonsense town hall-type forums in our lounge. We've stripped our dilemma down to its component parts, examined them one by one, put the dilemma back together, and considered the whole of it in both practical and impractical terms without quite managing to reach an official decision. As of the day this manuscript went off to the publisher —late, as usual—Joan and I honestly aren't certain that we want to return to our sublet apartment, our sublet fishing camp, and our sublet season football tickets in New York in July of 1975, as originally planned.

Certainly the despairing shape of the news from home hasn't inspired us to hurry back. It comes up the Atlantic jetstream, rises, shuffles through the Royal Mailmongers at Heathrow, and finds us, often at the worst possible moment. Any time we actually get to thinking we'd better readjust to right-hand traffic jams, 25¢ oranges and the chronic wail of police sirens in the night, another blast of downbeat correspondence turns the blood cold down in my rusty arteries. Maybe it's fate.

For instance, I actually had commenced composing a wheedling letter reminding the headmaster of a very good, very pricey Manhattan school of his dated promise to enroll Scott on our return, when an ominous flutter of inbound mail stayed my hand. The theme: the wonderful old bottom-line matter of bottom lines, prices, inflation of. Since I've been known to consume both in big league quantities, word that the price of the daily *New York Times* hit a high of 20¢ and packaged bread 60¢ put a permanent dent in my good nature.

"No matter what the Bureau of Labor Statistics and the rest of the feds say about inflation running only 12 to 15 percent a year—*only*, how does that grab you?—I personally say the cost of food, rent, entertainment, garage space, juice for the car, and other essentials has blown up 35 to 40 percent in Manhattan just this last year," a sample letter from a crank who used to share my binoculars as well as my smokes at Giant games reported.

If anything, the prevailing view among Wall Streeters with whom I once spent something more negotiable than my time— call it a character defect, but some of my best friends happen to be stockbrokers—wasn't what could be described exactly as the usual long-term growth situation bombast. An especially lugubrious letter from an erstwhile high-roller whose stricken current circumstances forced him to liquidate the chauffeur and drophead Bentley he'd laid on back when the Dow Jones numbers were running up around 1,000 conjured up visions of vested types taking practice jumps out of ground-floor windows downtown.

The market tables have been equally bearish in England lately, even a bit more bearish, in fact—Hail Gustave Levy, full of grace —but at least we've been able to warm ourselves on some economic bonanzas no longer possible in America. At approximately the time my Wall Street friend went to pieces in the letter he wouldn't want his diminishing customer list to see, I uncovered a handyman named Billy who agreed to treat a number of minor aches and pains around our digs. First day on the job he cut the grass, repaired a front door lock we seldom use, filled chinks in our stone wall with flowers, rehung a gate, sanded and painted an iron fence, reglazed two windows, mended the carpet sweeper, sunk iron clothesline posts in the back garden, patched a blowout in my bike, went skirling up a ladder to clean, patch, and replace one of the eaves, and otherwise worked like the nine furies despite Joan's solicitous suggestions that he call an occasional time out.

Stiffly, the pride of the old craftsman audible in his rural accents, he refused to accept any more than his usual full day rate of two pounds, or $5 U.S., although I did persuade him to take several packs of cigarettes, which he smoked like that Con Ed chimney on East Fourteenth Street while he worked. Hardworking, wonderfully unreasonable Players like Billy can't help but make a visiting American seriously consider leaning on that forwarding address for another year or so.

With newscasts consisting of little else, I'm all too aware of the fact that, by the numbers, general prices are inflating faster in Old Blighty right now. But since the relative base is pegged to a far more modest scale, my shirtsleeve calibrations tell me that even if current U.S. trends persist, which I prayerfully hope they won't, for the sake of consumers in both the mother country and the backslid colony, it will take another five years before a state of parity exists and we're all of us going up the road to the poorhouse together.

Besides runaway prices, frequent travels through England and Europe, and two family cars—we recently added an old number whose engine is signed Rolls-Royce—the big joints of prime meat that rule on our carving board, abundant domestic help, entertainment and change of clothes, and leased trout and salmon waters in which I regularly indulge my kinky whim only put us $712 U.S. over the $11,600 U.S. speed limit of our total annual budget the first full fiscal year.

What to do?

Along with the doomful economic forecasts from home, crime figures compiled by the FBI and thoughtfully sent along by an old fraternity brother had an ominous ring to them. On an across-the-board basis, lawlessness in 1973 went up by a roaring 15 percent over the identical quarter of the previous year, the blotter showing an even greater bulge of everything, including murder, or what a New York cop I know calls The Hit Parade, in communities of less than ten thousand population, which ought to give the racial bigots some pause, provided they can read.

At a distance of three thousand miles from all the action, however, crime figures can be rationalized as remote, numbers without names, the harvest of a whole nation, including especially noxious areas like Detroit, Chicago, Washington, and Dallas, which are far from New York. Or at least they could until the latest Bulletin of the Parents League of New York came sailing in from zip code 10021 to put a close-up focus on the situation. Teach Your Child Self-Defense, an advertisement for the Richard Chun Karate Center up on First Avenue screamed. My skin tightened some.

Then, just as I decided it was time to aim a mash note at the manic public relations executive in whose thrall I once sat to bashfully announce my candidacy for another term if the price was right—the mind boggles at what the right price must be with bread selling at 60¢—the impersonal crime figures came rapping at our very door. As a well-informed source described the incident, one night a couple who've lived in our apartment building on East Seventy-first Street almost for as long a time as we awaited the elevator after safely coming home to the protective sanctuary of the lobby. Out of nowhere there appeared a self-employed free-enterprise wonk presumably anxious to run up a stake for his connection. Holding a knife to the wife's wishbone, stating his needs in a dead flat tone, he stripped them of everything Uncle Moe the Friendly Pawnbroker issued tickets on, right down to their wedding rings. The crime wave couldn't lap any closer to home than that.

But basic baggage relevant to what currently passes as the good life is in no way confined to America's inflating price levels, inflating police blotters, inflating pollution muffling the sunshine, inflating lack of confidence in mandated leaders—needless to say, for cause—inflating pressure points between rich and poor, young and old, blacks, browns, greens, blues, and whites. Like it or not, there's more to existence.

Apart from Joan and my contentment in the soft slow English countryside, we have another consideration, our son, Scott, seven years old, healthy and happy; fond of swimming, fishing, horses, and wheeling a gleaming new bike along one-track rural roads; enthralled as his teachers open magical new doors on reading, writing, and what they call sums; whose face lights up when he kicks a soccer ball with other youngsters, inspects dinosaur fossil bones in the museums, spins the television dial in search of a dreadful stew called "Sale of the Century."

"Don't wrap your boy in cotton," a sweet, irascible friend conscripted as one of Scott's godfathers scolded us before we left for England. "It's important to expose him to the realities."

In New York City we inhabit an apartment decorated largely by the Mosler Safe Company, send Scott to a private school not nearly as polyglot as the local population, and flee the urban sprawl for weekends at a cabin deep in the country—the same as our advice-giving friend and most other acquaintances do. How's that for realities?

So far the two-room village school in Lower Slaughter is even more impressive than we'd been led to believe by an especially close writer chum, gone now, God bless him, who told us he'd found the village school in Kent, where his family did a memorable tour abroad, at least a year up on the highly regarded school system in Wilton, Connecticut, where his daughter attended class before and after their sojourn. Now that another no-nonsense year of English schooling is well underway for Scott, I'm convinced that gaudy testimonial was no exaggeration.

In addition to the regular course of study, Scott has even managed some extracurriculars in ripe old Elizabethan flavors thanks to several farmboy classmates who don't consciously restrict their vocabularies out of respect to a resident young Yank. One bittersweet afternoon Scott raised his voice to the decibel count of a television commercial, proudly looked me straight in the eye, and declared, "Daddy, I'm going upstairs to *have* a piss," indicating he'd got the tune, if not the exact lyrics. Could that be the sort of thing my friend meant by realities?

Back in real-world New York City I often fell to wondering about what struck me as a fairly jaded sense of values among Scott's peer group, who seemed a breed apart just by the look of them—gray, pinch-faced kids, little old men and women without sufficient laughter to them. To focus on merely one aspect of their blasé lives, they cross-fertilize at frequent birthday parties, splashy affairs, many of them, featuring Jiggs the Chimp, a frequent television performer able to ride a trick bike, smoke cigarettes, and snap photos. One of the parties was staged in the sacred preserve of the River Club, with forty—that's right, forty—youngsters treated to a sitdown meal, hired entertainment, and four separate gifts for themselves from FAO Schwarz, which isn't quite the way I remember birthdays in my own lost youth.

Wanting to do no less when it came time for our son's fifth

175

birthday, we organized much the same sort of a party, with decorations, catered sandwiches, ice cream, and cake, what ho-hum New York youngsters on the same track we run call loot bags stuffed with the bounty of the Mary Arnold Toy Store around the corner, and even a professional clown/guitarist reportedly a smash hit with subteens, whose fee for a brief matinee appearance came to exactly $35.

But by that time Scott and his playmates had been exposed to such a cornucopia of wonders that anything less than a live moon launch from our parlor was doomed to be more of the same old stuff. My first belated glimmer that this was so occurred during a market research investigation in mid-performance. Instead of being bombarded with the socko laughter and applause Smith and Dale used to receive at the Palace, the clown/guitarist was rolling up total silence, which is to put it mildly.

"He's a bore, isn't he?" one nice little girl, a terribly aging five, loudly told me in what I considered a breach of good manners, since I had underwritten and staged the extravaganza.

Faced with outright revolt—I can think of nothing more humiliating for a professional entertainer bagged up in a clown suit, singing and chording on a guitar, than to lose a captive audience of five-year-olds—the mummer desperately resorted to all manner of special effects, including a bulb horn to honk. But he'd lost them, he'd really lost them, and once gymnastics threatened to begin on some seventeenth-century furniture it seemed prudent to run down the curtain and pack the guests into the dining room for three-star vittles.

Just as everyone got a good grip on the finger sandwiches, the resident clown whose hourly wage came to more than my own, still suffering the humiliation up front, burst into the room all singsong and ho-ho laughter in a valiant effort to establish—reestablish is hardly the right word here—his tattered professional reputation. Instantly a boy at the end of the table rolled his eyeballs in one of those Dear God looks, and the celebrant himself enunciated what seemed the prevailing sentiments: "Oh, no, not again."

A year to the day later, Scott achieved his sixth birthday at our cottage in Lower Slaughter. No loot bags, no vaudeville, no red-assed chimp smoking what is said to be a health hazard, intruded on what I considered a far more appropriate, more blissful scene. Seven friends drawn from the school and the near village played games like pin-the-tail, piped Happy Birthday when the cake was brought out, and ate everything in sight. Unless I badly misread what my eyes and ears kept telling me, there was more genuine joy, more genuine laughter, and more wide-eyed excitement at that homemade party than at any of the catered overprivileged affairs I used to collect him from in Manhattan.

The attendant facts—that he has adjusted beautifully to the new geography; that he enjoys the run of the village after years on a short megalopolis leash, pelting over the landscape with friends for a close-up look at a swan gliding the stream, a new-born ewe feeding, or a combine harvest spinning a golden field; that he takes riding lessons without his sponsor worrying about the horse being mugged from under him—together have set us to reviewing our dilemma at a level we originally hadn't fully considered.

What to do, what to do?

Along with everything else, we haven't even felt the occasional flutter of homesickness we had half expected to. Personally, while almost every other stray bug in circulation is sure to find a home in my bloodstream, I haven't been susceptible to the hometown blues since a momentary lapse riding a goods train through the African night from Tabora to Mwadui in what was then Tanganyika in the autumn of 1948, although there are times when I wander lonely as a cloud brooding on some square-out pass pattern left behind in Shea Stadium.

It's perfectly true that I miss Tuesday night tennis up over Grand Central station, our jumbo copy of the *New York Times* outside the door each day, an endless choice of restaurants, theaters, films, museums, and sporting events. I miss Harriet, Pollard, Angelo, Steve, Dorothy and Brooks, Ray and Phyllis, Bob and Marge, Joe and Ginnie.

Sometimes we miss those and other American assets to a point of mild anguish, of course, but we haven't missed them enough to ring up the shipping people quite yet. Besides, it's not as if we're under canvas on the *Golden Hind* sailing beyond the rim of consciousness. After all, at current rates New York City is only 17½ ¢ U.S. away by air letter, $6 by phone, six-and-a-half hours on one of those big stainless steel birds, and four-and-a-half days by steamship. Whatever our ultimate decision, we expect to remain tuned to the proper wave lengths to keep up with friends, relatives, and the bittersweet passing scene back home.

This is not to say that we've swallowed the whole of the English life style without an occasional belch. We haven't. Every so often the sheeting rains, the drab colors of the day in need of a bright new coat of paint, national newspapers no bigger than the *Columbia Missourian* on which I cut my teeth, sticky British manners, clenched British accents, sausage rolls, Mind Your Head signs, and pubs forever named The Kings Arms, The White Swan, or The Duke of Wellington can and do become screamingly oppressive.

But mostly we like our brief exile beyond any singing of it. As I sit here typing the last of this a wood fire crackling in the grate puts a shine to the splendid old oak beam above us. Beyond our front windows the bowl of sky is salted with stars; the church steeple, slender and perfect, shows in a wedge of moonlight. An hour ago we fed on a bucket of Colonel Sanders I fetched back from a day in London, which proves it is possible to have the best of both worlds.

At times like this we can't help but wonder how long—psychologically, if not tactically—bone-deep Americans can remain abroad before renewing their subscription. Two years, three, four? The travel guides don't say.

As I sit typing the last of this we honestly haven't decided whether to return on schedule or stretch our foreign assignment a bit longer. The final decision is still very much up in the air, elusive, obscure, speculative, blurry, blowing in the wind, just like local weather conditions.

What to do, what to do, what to do?